GIVEON · SCARABS FROM RECENT EXCAVATIONS IN ISRAEL

ORBIS BIBLICUS ET ORIENTALIS

Published by the Biblical Institute of the University
of Fribourg Switzerland
the Seminar für Biblische Zeitgeschichte
of the University of Münster i. W. Federal Republic of Germany
and the Schweizerische Gesellschaft
für orientalische Altertumswissenschaft
Editor: Othmar Keel
Coeditors: Erich Zenger and Albert de Pury

ORBIS BIBLICUS ET ORIENTALIS 83

RAPHAEL GIVEON

SCARABS FROM RECENT EXCAVATIONS IN ISRAEL

edited by
David Warburton and Christoph Uehlinger

UNIVERSITÄTSVERLAG FREIBURG SCHWEIZ
VANDENHOECK & RUPRECHT GÖTTINGEN
1988

CIP-Titelaufnahme der Deutschen Bibliothek

Giveon Raphael:

Scarabs from recent excavations in Israel/Raphael Giveon. –
Freiburg, Schweiz: Univ-Verl.;
Göttingen: Vandenhoeck u. Ruprecht, 1988

   (Orbis biblicus et orientalis; 83)
   ISBN 3-525-53712-3 (Vandenhoeck & Ruprecht) Gb.
   ISBN 3-7278-0581-1 (Univ.-Verl.) Gb.
NE: GT

Publication subsidized by
the Swiss Academy
of Humanities

Die Druckvorlagen der Textseiten
wurden vom Autor ab Datenträger
als reprofertige Vorlage zur Verfügung gestellt.

© 1988 by Universitätsverlag Freiburg Schweiz
Vandenhoeck & Ruprecht Göttingen
Paulusdruckerei Freiburg Schweiz

ISBN 3-7278-0581-1 (Universitätsverlag)
ISBN 3-525-53712-3 (Vandenhoeck & Ruprecht)

Contents

Foreword   VII

Raphael Giveon ל"ז (1916-1985)   1
A Bibliography of Raphael Giveon   7

Scarabs and other Small Finds from Recent Excavations in Israel   17

The Catalogue System Employed   18

nos.	1-4	Tell Abu Zureiq	19
		A Note on the Recovery of these Scarabs, by Ezra Meyerhof	
	5-28	Achziv	22
	29-56	Tel Aphek	40
	57-61	Tel Arad	56
	62	Khorbat ᶜErav	60
	63-64	Ḥanita	62
	65-90	Tell Jerishe	62
	91	Tel Kabri	78
	92	Khirbet Karkara	80
	93-108	Tel Lachish	80
	109	Matzuva	92
	110-119	Tel Michal	92
	120	Saᶜar	100
	121	Tel Shem	100
	122	Tel Yitzḥaqi	102

Abbreviations   104
Reference works cited   105

Index   111
     Motif Index   111
     Tufnell/Ward Design Classes   114
     Materials Index   114

Plates

Foreword

In 1981 I started a research project, approved by the Israel Departement of Antiquities and Museums and supported by the Swiss National Science Foundation, which aims at the complete publication of Bronze and Iron Age stamp seals excavated in Palestine and Israel. Prof. Raphael Giveon had then the publication rights for a considerable number of such objects, and I therefore asked him to publish these as quickly as possible in order to make available this important material for our comprehensive corpus. Prof. Giveon kindly agreed and was able to publish a major part of it in his last two books which have appeared in 1985 ("Egyptian Scarabs from Western Asia from the Collections of the British Museum") and 1986 ("Egyptian Scarabs and Seals from Acco", together with Mrs. Trude Kertesz).

The third and most important volume of this series was planned to contain scarabs and other small finds of Egyptian origin which had been found during recent archaeological excavations in Israel directed by members of the Institute of Archaeology of Tel-Aviv University. Due to his sudden death, Prof. Giveon could no more complete this publication. We are most grateful to Mrs. Miriam Aharoni (Tel Arad), Dr. Zeev Herzog (Tell Jerishe, Tel Michal), Prof. Moshe Kochavi (Tel Aphek) and Prof. David Ussishkin (Tel Lachish) to have nevertheless made available their important finds for the present publication and to have given us the necessary informations concerning provenance and stratigraphy.

Through the generosity of Dr. M.W. Prausnitz, it was also possible to include an important group of excavated scarabs and stamp seals from Achziv studied since long by Prof. Giveon. Finally, we could add some scarabs which had been excavated or picked up at smaller sites and which come mostly from various kibbutzim or private collections.

Prof. Giveon's study of these objects had been left in a quite uneven state of research at the time of his death. If some few parts were almost ready for publication (Tel Michal), only preliminary handwritten notes were available for other parts. Thanks to the help of Mrs. Yehudit Giveon-Genzer and Prof. Raphael Ventura, all the notes and manuscripts could be collected. The Institute of Archaeology of Tel-Aviv University agreed to have the whole material photographed by Mr. S. Weinberg and drawn by Mrs. Rodika Penchas. It remained then the work of David Warburton, Christoph Uehlinger and myself to bring the catalogue at a more or less uniform level of research. The typing of the almost definite manuscript was done by Anastasia Bernet.

Due to the untimely death of Raphael Giveon, his third book on scarabs has become a memorial volume. A short biography and a bibliography, compiled by Naama Azulay, therefore open the present volume.

The now finished catalogue can no more allow to distinguish clearly between excavators' informations, insights of Raphael Giveon and additions of the various other contributors: this should be so, as such a rich harvest had suddenly become a heritage.

Othmar Keel

VII

Raphael Giveon ז"ל (1916-1985)

Raphael Giveon was born on February 8, 1916 in the industrial municipality of Elberfeld in Rhenish Palatinate, today in the Federal Republic of Germany. His parents, Louis and Sophie Grüneberg, were members of the strongly assimilated Jewish middle class, his father being a merchant. The child, the last-born of three, received the name of Richard Grüneberg. Of this German name, only the initials remain in his Hebrew one which he took in 1948 at the foundation of the state of Israel.

Since 1929 Elberfeld was, together with other industrial municipalities, a part of the larger agglomeration of Wuppertal. For this reason Raphael Giveon, when asked for his place of birth, sometimes indicated Elberfeld, sometimes Wuppertal. In Elberfeld-Wuppertal he went to primary school and college. At that time he was interested above all in natural sciences, especially Botany. During walks in the Swiss alps in the 1980's he could still amaze me with his knowledge of plants, and he was still able to identify many flowers by their latin names. He is said to have discovered, during one of his botanical excursions, a stalactite cave in the vicinity of Wuppertal.

As of 1933 Jews were excluded from German colleges. Richard Grüneberg moved to Berlin where he went to the famous "Hochschule für die Wissenschaft des Judentums". At the same time he worked in agriculture: soon after his arrival in Berlin he had joined the Zionist youth organization Ha-Shomer Ha-Za^cir which, through agricultural training, prepared young Jews for emigration to Palestine. Richard advanced quickly to a leading position and organized emigration in increasingly difficult conditions. In this connection he had to travel illegally several times from Berlin to Vienna. He later told me that the situation in Berlin, however difficult, was marked by the correct application of an increasingly draconic legislation but that Vienna was dominated by an anti-semitic zeal which made his work almost impossible. It was during one of his stays in Vienna that he came to know his later wife Yehudit Genzer.

Shortly before the war began, he accompanied a group of young people to Palestine. He then returned to England in order to organize Zionist youth work there and was surprised by the outbreak of the war. After Britain joined the war he was put in

1

an internment camp for a year since he was a German citizen. It was then that he became interested for the first time in the study of the Hebrew Bible as an historical book. When he left the camp he worked as a teacher. This furthered his interest in developmental psychology and pedagogy. Education and training, the intercourse with children and youths were always more than a troublesome burden for him. His ever awake curiosity and his open-minded and totally undogmatical manner always let him find easy contact with the younger generations.

Two days after the end of the war - Richard's parents had succumbed to the in-human conditions in the concentration camp of Theresienstadt - he left England together with his wife Yehudit, whom he had married in 1944, and went to settle down in Palestine. Both went to the Kibbutz Mishmar Ha-ᶜEmeq which had been founded in 1926 in the forest region between Haifa and Megiddo on the north-eastern slope of the Carmel. The kibbutz was a training centre of the leftist Ha-Shomer Ha-Zaᶜir movement, and Raphael could continue his teaching activities there. Soon he also acted as a teacher at the kibbutz movements' training centre of Oranim near Haifa, first in English, then in Hebrew. In 1947 Raphael and Yehudit became members of the kibbutz Mishmar Ha-ᶜEmeq. The couple had two girls, born in 1951 and 1953 respectively.

Soon thereafter, he was seized by the national passion of archaeology. However, the hard conditions of the pioneers' time did not allow much for such luxuries as archaeological studies. Raphael changed from teaching to agriculture in order to have more leisure time and to do private studies in archaeology. He soon volunteered for night-watch and so could participate in archaeological excavations during the day-time.

With all his love for Israel he was never a narrow-minded nationalist, and he realized very soon how ancient Israel had been bound into multiple relations with other countries. He was therefore interested in its neighbouring cultures, above all in Egypt which had impressed its influence on Israel in the most visible way. It was only in Jerusalem that one could study Egyptology at that time. To attend the introduction to Hieroglyphics by the world-famous linguist Hans Jacob Polotsky who was teaching at the Hebrew University since 1934 but became a professor only in 1948, Raphael had to get up at four a.m., hitch-hike in cold rain or burning *ḥamsin* to Jerusalem, come back by hitch-hiking to the kibbutz and then change clothes right on the field in order to do his share of agricultural work.

So much enthusiasm and sacrifice could not leave the kibbutz community un-impressed. In 1959 he was allowed to do regular studies in Egyptology in Paris where he went to courses, seminars and exercises at the Ecole Pratique des Hautes Etudes, the Collège de France, and the Sorbonne. It was there that he got acquainted

2

with the Egyptian egyptologist Labib Habachi (+ 18.2.1984) who was 10 years older than he, and with whom he had a deep friendship inspite of all the then dominating political hostilities. This episode is rather typical for Raphael's open-minded will to reconciliation.

His doctoral thesis, which he did under the direction of Prof. Georges Posener and in continual contact with Jean Yoyotte, was concerned with the *Š3sw*, an ethnical group whose main living area had been in southern Jordan and Sinai where they probably lived as nomads. The *Š3sw* are attested to as an ethnical entity mainly in sources of the New Kingdom. Later the term *Š3sw* became a professional terminus for "herdsman". The aim of Raphael's dissertation was to collect all the sources mentioning this problematic entity and to evaluate them with respect to the history of Egypt and of the southern borders of Palestine. As the sources of the 14th century B.C.E. mention a country (of the god) *jhw* in connection with the *Š3sw*, it is rather probable that at least some of the latter did worship a god who was a prototype of YHWH, the later protective deity of the tribes of Israel. The *Š3sw* represent one element from which at least some groups converged to the later tribal confederacy of Israel.

In 1961 Raphael returned to Israel with his doctoral title. It was only ten years later that the thesis was published by Brill in Leyden as "Les bédouins Shosou des documents égyptiens". Raphael was the first member of the kibbutz Mishmar Ha-ᶜEmeq to have completed an academic degree and probably one of the first kibbutzniks at all to do this. This way of life which is so typical for Israel was then still much marked by the struggle to survive and by agriculture, and there was not much comprehension for the desire to study such a specialized field as Egyptology. Only with the combination of self-esteem and understanding the others' position, which was so typical for Raphael, could one manage to realize such an aim without leaving the kibbutz.

Soon after his return from Paris he was called by Prof. Shmuel Yeivin (1896-1982) as a lecturer in the Department of Ancient Near Eastern Civilizations of Tel Aviv University. In 1968, when Yohanan Aharoni (1919-1976) took over the directorship of the Department, it was renamed the Department of Archaeology and Ancient Near Eastern Cultures. There Raphael worked during some twenty years until his retirement in 1984, and still later, as his own substitute, during the academic year 1984/1985. His teaching activity had won much interest since Egypt had become the first neighbouring state to become accessible to Israelis in the aftermath of A. Sadat's spectacular visit on November 19-20, 1977, and after the peace treaty of March 16, 1979. Raphael was one of the first Israelis to visit Egypt, and he led the first Academic Tour of Egyptian Antiquities.

During most of the time of his scientific activity, however, access to the Egyptian monuments was either not possible or rather difficult. The nearest museum with Egyptian antiquities was some three flight hours away in Torino, and Egyptologists from abroad mostly avoided the Zionist state in order not to become compromised with Egypt. Israeli Egyptology was limited by these exterior conditions, as well as by the special direction given through the work of its dean Polotsky, almost exclusively to the philological and linguistic field. Raphael was one of the few Egyptologists who concentrated on a field with specific interest for the history and archaeology of Israel, namely the study of Egypto-Palestinian relations based upon objects of Egyptian origin or influence discovered in local excavations in Israel.

Once it had become known that *ḥaver* Giveon was doing Egyptology, other kibbutzniks, who had found a scarab or an amulet while looking around on a neighbouring tell, turned to him for an explanation of what chance had offered them. Raphael's bibliography testifies to his early interest in such accidental discoveries, which have often been of considerable scholarly interest. Besides the harmless shabbat tourists and kibbutzniks, also systematic collectors of antiquities such as Moshe Dayan or Reuben Hecht often asked Raphael for his opinion to identify and evaluate ancient artifacts of Egyptian origin and to decipher their inscription or to interpret the meaning of their decoration and iconography. He responded enthusiastically to their requests, since they gave him the opportunity to study objects whose existence might otherwise remain unknown to scholars.

Raphael's most important correspondents in this field, however, were of course numerous archaeological expeditions which offered him their Egyptian and Egyptianizing finds for publication. It is just such material that will be presented in the present volume. Raphael's interest in Egyptian stamp seals, especially scarabs which mirror in such a particularly interesting way the relations of Egypt and Palestine from the Middle Kingdom down to the Iron Age, has led to several major publications, the present book being the last one of the series. A summary of his far-reaching knowledge in this field appeared in the article "Skarabäus" in the *Lexikon der Ägyptologie*.

One of Raphael's most important projects during the years when the Sinai was under Israeli control was the study and preservation of the remains at Serabit el-Khadem, the ancient Egyptian turquoise mining center in southern Sinai particularly famous for its inscriptions in the so-called Proto-Sinaitic alphabetic script. He was not allowed to excavate there but made many valuable discoveries nevertheless. His studies then were greatly furthered by his acquaintance with Moshe Dayan, then Defence Minister, who supported him with all kinds of technical material. With his so typical and agreeable ability to laugh about himself, Raphael often told us how he should have photographed Serabit while helplessly dangling from a flying heli-copter. He was much better with the Beduin people sitting around a camp-fire after a day's work. He had already imagined a title for the publication that should include his discoveries in the area of Serabit; with reference to the famous work of Gardiner and Peet, "Inscriptions of Sinai", his own should be named "Additional Inscriptions of Sinai". It will now be the task of his student Raphael Ventura to bring this already advanced work to a good end.

After the peace treaty was signed with Egypt, Raphael's hope was to start a major excavation project in the Egyptian Delta and thus be able to advance from the occu-pation with small Egyptian objects to the study of greater monuments in the Egyp-tian heartland. Sadly this will no longer be possible.

Besides trying to bring Israeli Egyptology nearer to the Egyptian monuments themselves, Raphael was also engaged in establishing ties with international Egyp-tology. Studies in Paris, sabbatical leaves in Oxford, numerous guest lectures in many European countries and his participation in almost all major congresses on Egyptology, where he often presented papers about his newest discoveries, allowed him to bind Israeli archaeology nearer to the international community of Egypto-logists. As he never thought of his field as of an academic caste system, not only his own students but also students and assistants all around the world took benefit from his ability to make contacts. His untamable curiosity, his desire to always extend his horizons (be it in culinary matters) and his ability to enjoy made him an agreeable and always much esteemed guest. His huge correspondence testifies to his interest in the research of other colleagues as well as to his promptness in sharing his knowledge without any jealousy or avarice. His self-esteem, which was the foundation of his esteem for the others, demanded that this knowledge should be communicated under his name, but he was never anxious nor paltry in such matters.

By his death on August 8, 1985 in the District Hospital of Afula, Raphael has been taken out of an unrestricted participation in the life of the international com-munity of Egyptologists. His quick presentation of Egyptian finds, which come to light in almost every season of excavations in Israel, his human warmth and friendly cooperation leave a breach that will be long felt. Trying to go the way he has shown is the adequate manner of working through the grief.

Othmar Keel *

* I am especially grateful to Mrs. Yehudit Giveon-Genzer and to Prof. Raphael Ventura for having supplied me information about the life and work of Prof. Raphael Giveon.

A Bibliography of Raphael Giveon

compiled by
Naama Azulay

I - BOOKS

1969

(1) (1) מאוצרות מצרים העתיקה בישראל (קטלוג) . בית וילפריד.
קבוץ הזורע. 129. עמ' 3, לוחות צילומים.

1971

(2) Les bédouins Shosou des documents égyptiens (Documenta et monumenta Orientis antiqui 18), Leiden, 278 pp., 29 pls.

1974

(3) (3) עקבות פרעה בכנען . קובץ מאמרים על קשרי ארץ־ישראל ומצרים
העתיקה. הוצאת המדור לידיעת הארץ בתנועה הקיבוצית.תל־אביב תשל"ד
188. עמ' , ציורים , צלומים.

(4) The Stones of Sinai Speak [in Japanese], Tokyo, 208 pp., pls. and ills.

1978

(5) The Impact of Egypt on Canaan. Iconographical and Related Studies (Orbis Biblicus et Orientalis 20), Fribourg/Switzerland and Göttingen, 132 pp., pls. and ills.

(6) The Stones of Sinai Speak, Tokyo, 164 pp., pls. and ills.

1983

(7) (7) אבני סיני .מוסד ביאליק ירושלים תשמ"ג. 171. עמ' 3 , מפות , 16
לוחות תמונות.

1985

(8) Egyptian Scarabs from Western Asia from the Collections of the British Museum (Orbis Biblicus et Orientalis. Series Archaeologica 3), Fribourg/Switzerland and Göttingen, 202 pp., pls. and ills.

1986

(9) [With Trude KERTESZ] Egyptian Scarabs and Seals from Acco. From the Collections of the Israel Department of Antiquities and Museums, Fribourg/Switzerland, 48 pp., 20 pls.

7

II - ARTICLES

1955

(10) צפרדעים כמתנת קבורה (Frogs as Burial Offerings) : ידיעות החברה (10)
לחקירת ארץ־ישראל ועתיקותיה י"ט תשט"ו עמ' 238-239.

1957

(11) In the Valley of Megiddon (Zech. XII:11): JJS 8, pp. 155-163.

1959

(12) חרפושית מתל נגילה (ממצא חדש מאוסף רוחמה) A Plaque) (12)
טבע וארץ ב' תש"ך עמ' 137 + 140 (= pp. 88-89, Book no. 5).‏ from Tel Nagila)
(13) King or God on the Sarcophagus of Ahiram: IEJ 9, pp. 57-59 (= 5, pp. 31-33).

1961

(14) חותמת מצרית מכפר רופין (An Egyptian Seal from Kefar Ruppin) : (14)
ידיעות החברה לחקירת ארץ־ישראל ועתיקותיה כ"ה תשכ"א עמ' 249-250.
(15) Two New Hebrew Seals and their Iconographic Background: PEQ 93, pp. 38-42 (= book no. 5, pp. 110-116).

1962

(16) שלשה שרידים עתיקים (Three Ancient Objects) : טבע וארץ ד' (16)
תשכ"ב עמ' 312-317.
(17) A Ramesside 'Semitic' Letter: RSO 37, pp. 167-173.

1963

(18) פסל מצרי מסביבות עין השופט An Egyptian Statuette from the) (18)
ידיעות החברה לחקירת ארץ־ישראל ועתיקותיה (Vicinity of ᶜEin Ha-Shofet
כ"ז תשכ"ג עמ' 293-295 (= Book no. 5, pp. 28-30).
(19) A Ptolemaic Fayence Bowl: IEJ 13, pp. 20-29.

1964

(20) שלש חרפושיות מלכותיות מתל צפית Three Royal Scarabs from) (20)
טבע וארץ ז' תשכ"ד עמ' 79-81 (= Book no. 5, pp. 99-104).‏ (Tel Zafit
(21) Alexandrine Decorated Basin-Rims from Israel: IEJ 14, pp. 232-236.
(22) The Cities of our God: II Sam. 10,12: JBL 83, pp. 415-416.
(23) Toponymes ouest-asiatiques à Soleb: VT 14, pp. 239-255.

1965

(24) A Sealing of Khyan from the Shephela of Southern Palestine: JEA 51, pp. 202-204
(25) Two Egyptian Documents concerning Bashan from the Time of Ramses II: RSO 40, pp. 197-202.

8

1967

(26) Three Fragments of Statuary) שְׁלֹשָׁה קִטְעֵי פְּסָלִים מִן הַשָּׁרוֹן הַצְּפוֹנִי (26)
(from the Northern Sharon : יְדִיעוֹת הַחֶבְרָה לַחֲקִירַת אֶרֶץ-יִשְׂרָאֵל וְעַתִּיקוֹתֶיהָ
ל"א תשכ"ז עמ' 118-123.

(27) תְּעוּדוֹת וּשְׂרִידִים מִצְרִיִּים כְּחוֹמֶר לְתוֹלְדוֹת הָעֵמֶק הַמַּעֲרָבִי (27)
(Egyptian Documents and Objects as Material for the History of the Western
Esdraelon Valley) : סֵפֶר הָעֵמֶק – מֵאֶרֶץ קִישׁוֹן תשכ"ל עמ' 163-169.

(28) Ptah and Astarte on a Seal from Acco, in: Studi sull'Oriente e la Bibbia offerti
a P. Giovanni Rinaldi, Genova, pp. 147-153 (= **5**, pp. 90-96).

(29) Royal Seals of the XIIth Dynasty from Western Asia: RdE 19, pp. 29-37 (=
book no. **5**, pp. 73-80).

(30) The Shosu of Egyptian Sources and the Exodus, in: Proceedings of the Fourth
World Congress of Jewish Studies. Vol. I, Jerusalem, pp. 193-196.

1968

(31) חוֹתָמוֹת מִצְרִיִּים – רְכִישׁוֹת חֲדָשׁוֹת שֶׁל הַמּוּזֵיאוֹן יַמִּיָּה בְּחֵיפָה (31)
(Egyptian Seals. New Acquisitions of the Maritime Museum, Haifa) : סְפוֹנִים ב'
תשכ"ח עמ' 62-63 (= Book no. **5**, pp. 105-106).

(32) An Alexandrine Basin-Rim from Ascalon: IEJ 18, p. 247.

(33) Egyptian Tomb-Scenes on Phoenician Objects from the Near East and from
Spain: Archivo Español de Arqueología 41, pp. 5-15.

(34) The Egyptian Funerary Cones at the Israel Museum: The Israel Museum
News 3, pp. 40-41.

(35) Quelques rencontres personnelles avec des antiquités en Israël: Cahiers
Numismatiques 16, pp. 528-535.

1969

(36) הַמִּקְדָּשׁ בְּסֵרַאבִּיט אֶל חַ'אדֶם (The Temple at Serabit el-Khadem) :
טֶבַע וָאָרֶץ י"א תשכ"ט עמ' 167-173.

(37) חוֹתָמוֹת וְקֻמְעוֹת מִתֵּל חַלִיף (Seals and Amulets from Tel Ḥalif) :
נִסְפָּח לַמַּאֲמָר : א. בִּירָן וֵר. גוֹפְנָא, מְעָרוֹת קְבָרִים מִתְקוּפַת הַבַּרְזֶל בְּתֵל
חַלִיף: אֶרֶץ-יִשְׂרָאֵל י"ט (סֵפֶר אוֹלְבְּרַייט) תשכ"ט עמ' 32-38.

(38) Egyptian Inscriptions and Finds from a Temple in the Timna Area, in: Proceedings of the Vth World Congress of Jewish Studies, Jerusalem, vol. I, pp. 50-53.

(39) Thutmosis IV and Asia: JNES 28, pp. 54-59.

1970

(40) שְׁלֹשָׁה פִּסְלֵי 'שׁוּבַתִּי' מִימֵי הַשּׁוֹשֶׁלֶת הַמִּצְרִית הכ"ו בְּיִשְׂרָאֵל (40)
(Three 'Shauabti' Figurines of the XXVIth Dynasty from Israel) : סֵפֶר שְׁמוּאֵל
יֵיבִּין . יְרוּשָׁלַיִם תשל"ל עמ' 342-350.

(41) The Shosou of the Late XXth Dynasty: JARCE 8 (1969-70) pp. 51-53.

9

1971

(42) מקדש חתחור בסראביט אל ח'אדם (The Temple of Hathor at Serabit el-Khadem) : קדמוניות ד' תשל"א עמ' 18-14.

(43) שנהבים בתקופה הישראלית : שנהבי שומרון (Ivories from the Israelite Period: the Samaria Ivories) שומרון – לקט מאמרים ומקורות, הוצאת המדור לידיעת הארץ בתנועה הקיבוצית תשל"א עמ' 99-88 (= ,Book no. 5) pp. 34-44.

1972

(44) חתחור כאלת הנגינה בסיני (Hathor as the Goddess of Music in Sinai) : תצליל 6 תשל"ב עמ' 9-5 (= 72-68 .Book no. 5, pp).

(45) An Egyptian Official in Gezer?: IEJ 22, pp. 143-144.

(46) Egyptian Temples in Canaan: Museum Ha'aretz, Tel-Aviv. Bulletin 14, pp. 57-62 (= book no. 5, pp. 22-27).

(47) Le temple d'Hathor à Serabit el-Khadem: Archaeologia 44, pp. 64-69.

1973

(48) כתובות מצריות מאוסף משה דיין (Egyptian Inscriptions from the Dayan Antiquities Collection) : בתוך י. אהרוני (עורך), חפירות ומחקרים מוגש לפרופסור שמואל ייבין. תל אביב תשל"ג עמ' 182-177.

(49) Egyptian Objects in Bronze and Fayence, in: Y. AHARONI, ed., Beer-Sheba I, Tel-Aviv, pp. 54-55.

1974

(50) החרפושיות מגנוסר (The Scarabs from Ginnosar) : עתיקות ז' תשל"ד עמ' 42-40 (= 87-85 .Book no. 5, pp).

(51) [עם א. אורן] תבליט מצרי מימי הממלכה הקדומה בדרום סיני (An Old Kingdom Relief in Sinai) : קדמוניות ז' תשל"ד עמ' 101-98.

(52) Amenophis III in Athribis: GM 9, pp. 25-26.

(53) Determinatives of Canaanite Personal Names and Toponyms in Egyptian, in: A. CAQUOT/ D. COHEN, éds., Actes du Premier Congrès International de Linguistique Sémitique et Chamito-Sémitique (Paris, 16-19 juillet 1969), La Haye - Paris, pp. 55-59 (expanded in book no. 5, pp. 15-21).

(54) Egyptian Objects from Sinai in the Australian Museum: AJBA 2, pp. 29-47.

(55) Hyksos Scarabs with Names of Kings and Officials from Canaan: ChdE 49, pp. 222-233.

(56) A Monogram Scarab from Tel Masos: Tel Aviv 1, pp. 75-76 (= book no. 5, pp. 107-109).

(57) Investigations in the Egyptian Mining Centres in Sinai: Tel Aviv 1, pp. 100-108.

(58) A Second Relief of Sekhemkhet in Sinai: BASOR 216, pp. 17-20.

1975

(59) בעלת הטורקיז – האלה חתחור בסראביט אל ח'אדם ובתמנע (59)
: (The Lady of the Turquoise. The Goddess Hathor at Serabit el-Khadem and Timna)
ארץ־ישראל י"ב (ספר נלסון גליק) תשל"ה עמ' 24-26 (= pp. 61-67, Book no. 5).

(60) A Late Egyptian Statue from the Eastern Delta: JARCE 12, pp. 19-21.

(61) A Late Ramesside Epithet of Thot: GM 17, pp. 23-25.

(62) The Scarabs, in: Y. AHARONI, ed., Investigations at Lachish (= Lachish V), Tel-Aviv, p. 71.

(63) Two Inscriptions of Ramesses II: IEJ 25, pp. 247-249.

1976

(64) תצליל : (An Ancient 'Mondscheinsonate') מזמור קדום לאור הירח (64)
9 תשל"ו עמ' 3-5 (= pp. 117-120, Book no. 5).

(65) Nakhman. A Personal Name with the Plant Determinative: RdE 28, pp. 155-156.

(66) New Egyptian Seals with Titles and Names from Canaan: Tel Aviv 3, pp. 127-133.

(67) Seals and Seal-Impressions of the XXVth Egyptian Dynasty in Western Asia: Revista de la Universidad Complutense 25 (Homenaje a Garcia Belido I), pp. 133-138 (= book no. 5, pp. 121-126).

(68) Some Scarabs Reconsidered: Archivo Español de Arquelogía 9, pp. 159-163.

(69) Two Critical Notes Concerning Sinai: GM 20, pp. 23-25.

1977

(70) נוסעים מימים עברו (Early Travellers) : נופים 8 תשל"ז עמ' 14-23. (70)

(71) The God) האל תות בסיני – פענוח שתי כתובות שנתגלו לאחרונה (71)
(Thoth in Sinai. Two Recently Discovered Inscriptions : נופים 8 תשל"ז עמ' 24-26.

(72) Egyptian Finger Rings and Seals from South of Gaza: Tel Aviv 4, pp. 66-70.

(73) Egyptology in Israel: GM 24, pp. 7-12.

(74) The Egyptian Objects, in: S. BEN-ARIEH/G. EDELSTEIN, Akko Tombs Near the Persion Gardens: ᶜAtiqot (Engl. Ser.) 12, pp. 70-71.

(75) Inscriptions of Sahureᶜ and Sesostris I from Wadi Khariğ (Sinai): BASOR 226, pp. 61-63.

(76) Remarks on the Transmission of Egyptian Lists of Asiatic Toponyms, in: J. ASSMANN/E. FEUCHT/R. GRIESHAMMER, Hrsg., Fragen an die Altägyptische Literatur. Studien zum Gedenken an Eberhard Otto, Wiesbaden, pp. 171-183.

1978

(77) A Group of Egyptian Amulets) קבוצת קמעות מצריות מכפר ערה (77)
(from Kefar ᶜAra) : אזור מנשה ז' תשל"ח מאמר מס. 5.

(78) Remarks on Ancient) לרשימות שמות מקומות מצריים עתיקים (78)
(Egyptian Toponym Lists : שנתון למקרא ולחקר המזרח הקדום ג' תשל"ט עמ' 124-128.

(79) Corrected Drawings of Sahure[c] and Sesostris I Inscriptions from the Wadi Khariğ: BASOR 232, p. 74.

(80) A Long Lost Inscription of Thutmosis IV: Tel Aviv 5, pp. 170-174.

(81) The XIIIth Dynasty in Asia: RdE 30, pp. 163-167.

(82) Two Unique Egyptian Inscriptions from Tel Aphek: Tel Aviv 5, pp. 188-191.

(83) Fouilles et Travaux de l'Université de Tel-Aviv. Découvertes égyptiennes récentes: BSFE 81, pp. 6-17.

1979

(84) Remarks on Some Egyptian Toponym Lists Concerning Canaan, in: M. GÖRG/E. PUSCH, Hrsg., Festschrift Elmar Edel (Ägypten und Altes Testament 1), Bamberg, pp. 135-141.

1980

(85) המצרים בסיני (The Egyptians in Sinai) : בתוך ז. משל וי. (85) פינקלשטיין (עורכים) : קדמוניות סיני . תל אביב תש"ם עמ' 313-320.

(86) A New Hyksos King: Tel Aviv 7, pp. 90-91.

(87) Some Scarabs from Canaan with Egyptian Titles: Tel Aviv 7, pp. 179-184.

1981

(88) שלושה קטעמי רשימות גאוגרפיות מצריות (Three Fragments from) (88) ארץ-ישראל ט"ו (ספר יוחנן אהרוני) תשמ"א : (Egyptian Geographical Lists עמ' 137-139.

(89) Ya[c]qob-har: GM 44, pp. 17-20.

(90) Geba[c] (Urk. IV 786,114): GM 49, pp. 33-35.

(91) A New Kingdom Stela from Sinai: IEJ 31, pp. 168-171.

(92) Some Egyptological Considerations Concerning Ugarit, in: G.D. YOUNG, ed., Ugarit in Retrospect, pp. 55-58.

1982

(93) התגלות האחרונה מסראביט אל ח'אדם (The Last Discovery from) (93) בתוך ז. משל וא. לכיש (עורכים) : מחקרי דרום סיני . תל : (Serabit el-Khadem אביב תשמ"ב עמ' 23-24.

(94) Asiatics in the Egyptian Mining Centres in South Sinai. Recent Discoveries: Middle East 1, pp. 37-40.

(95) A God Who Hears, in: M.H. VAN VOSS/D.J. HOEMS/G. MUSSIES/D. VAN DER PLAS/H. TE VELDE, eds., Studies in Egyptian Religion. Dedicated to Professor Jan Zandee, Leiden, pp. 38-42.

(96) Gold and Silver in Sinai. A Correction: GM 59, p. 103.

(97) Western Asiatic Aspects of the Amarna Period. The Monotheism Problem, in: L'égyptologie en 1979, Tome II, Paris, pp. 249-251.

1983

(98) A Second Look at Some Inscribed Scarabs: GM 67, pp. 33-37.

(99) A Date Corrected: If it is Hebrew to you: GM 69, p. 95.

(100) The Hyksos in the South, in: Fontes atque Pontes. Eine Festgabe für Hellmut Brunner (Ägypten und Altes Testament 5), Wiesbaden, pp. 155-161.

(101) Two Officials of the Old Kingdom at Magharah (Southern Sinai): Tel Aviv 10, pp. 49-51.

(102) An Inscription of Ramses III from Lachish: Tel Aviv 10, pp. 176-177.

(103) [With A. KEMPINSKI] The Scarabs, in: V. FRITZ/A. KEMPINSKI, Hrsg., Die Ergebnisse der Ausgrabungen auf der Ḥirbet el-Mšaš (Tel Masos), Vol. I, Wiesbaden, pp. 102-105.

1984

(104) בתוך : (An Egyptian Tablet from Shunam) לוחית מצרית משונם (104)
א. שילר (עורך) : ספר זאב וילנאי . ירושלים תשמ"ד עמ' 230-231.

(105) Amenmesse in Canaan?: GM 83, pp. 27-29.

(106) Archaeological Evidence for the Exodus: Bulletin of the Anglo-Israel Archaeological Society 1983/84, pp. 42-44.

(107) Geva. A New Fortress City from Thutmosis to Herod: Bulletin of the Anglo-Israel Archaeological Society 1983/84, pp. 45-46.

(108) A Middle Kingdom Statue from Serabit el-Khadim in Sinai: IEJ 34, pp. 154-155.

(109) Soped in Sinai, in: Studien zu Sprache und Religion Ägyptens (Festschrift W. Westendorf), Band II, Göttingen, pp. 777-784.

(110) A Canopic Figure from Roman Palestine, in: Mélanges Adolphe Gutbub, Montpellier.

1985

(111) Dating the Cape Gelidonya Shipwreck: AnSt 35, pp. 99-101.

1986

(112) New Material Concerning Canaanite Gods in Egypt: Proceedings of the IXth World Congress of Jewish Studies, Jerusalem, pp. 1-4.

III - ARTICLES IN ENYCLOPAEDIAS

1967

(113) האנציקלופדיה למדעי החברה , כרך ג' תל אביב תשכ"ז .
- מצרים העתיקה (Ancient Egypt) עמ' 658-668.

1971

(114) האנציקלופדיה העברית , כרך כ"ב תל אביב תש"ל .
- מזבח (Altar) עמ' 886-889.

13

1975

(115) Lexikon der Ägyptologie, hrsg. von W. HELCK und E. OTTO, Band I, Wiesbaden.
1. Amurru, col. 251-252. 2. Asdod, col. 462. 3. Asiaten, col. 462-471.
4. Askalon, col. 471-472.

1977

(116) Lexikon der Ägyptologie, hrsg. von W. HELCK und W. WESTENDORF, Band II, Wiesbaden.
5. Gaza, col. 381-383. 6. Hamath, col. 935-936. 7. Hapiru, col. 952-955.

1980

(117) Lexikon der Ägyptologie, hrsg. von W. HELCK und W. WESTENDORF, Band III, Wiesbaden.
8. Jam, col. 242-243. 9. Januammu, col. 244-245.
10. Libanon, col. 1013-1014. 11. Maghara, col. 1135-1137.

1982

(118) Lexikon der Ägyptologie, hrsg. von W. HELCK und W. WESTENDORF, Band IV, Wiesbaden.
12. Megiddo, col. 1-3. 13. Migdol, col. 124-125.
14. Nahr el-Kelb, col. 319-320. 15. Ortsnamenlisten, col. 621-622.
16. Palästina, col. 642-644. 17. Phönizien, col. 1039-1040.
18. Protosinaitische Inschriften, col. 1156-1159.

1984

(119) Lexikon der Ägyptologie, hrsg. von W. HELCK und W. WESTENDORF, Band V, Wiesbaden.
19. Rehob, col. 207-208. 20. Semqen, col. 847.
21. Serabit el-Chadim, col. 866-868. 22. Sichem, col. 922.
23. Sidon, col. 922-923. 24. Simyra, col. 947-948.
25. Sinai, col. 948-950. 26. Skarabäus, col. 968-981.
27. Sopdu, col. 1107-1110.

1986

(120) Lexikon der Ägyptologie, hrsg. von W. HELCK und W. WESTENDORF, Band VI, Wiesbaden.
28. Tachsi, col. 143-144. 29. Tempel, ägyptische in Kanaan, col. 357-358.
30. Thaanach, col. 462-463. 31. Timna, col. 593-595.
32. Tyrus, col. 817-820. 33. Ugarit, col. 838-842.
34. Ullaza, col. 842-843.

IV - REVIEW ARTICLES

1958

(121) Ivories from Nimrud and) שׁנהבי נימרוד ושׁנהבי ארץ־ישׂראל (121)
[Review : ידיעות החברה לחקירת ארץ־ישׂראל ועתיקותיה כ"ב (Ivories from Israel
article of R.D. BARNETT, A Catalogue of the Nimrud Ivories, London 1957.] .(Book no. 5, pp. 45-50 =) 55-61 עמ' תשׁי"ח

1973

(122) W.A. WARD, Egypt and the East Mediterranean World 2000-1900 B.C. Studies in Egyptian Foreign Relations During the First Intermediate Period, Beirut 1971: ChdE 48, pp. 88-92.

1976

(123) D. LORTON, The Juridical Terminology of International Relations in Egyptian Texts through Dyn. XVIII, Baltimore and London 1974: BiOr 33, col. 18-21.

1978

(124) A. NIBBI, The Sea Peoples. A Re-Examination of the Egyptian Sources, Oxford 1972; A. NIBBI, The Sea Peoples and Egypt, Park Ridge 1975: BiOr 35, col. 76-78.

1979

(125) A. HASSAN, Stöcke und Stäbe im pharaonischen Ägypten bis zum Ende des Neuen Reiches, München – Berlin 1976: ChdE 54, p. 93.

1980

(126) Resheph in Egypt. A Review Article on W.J. FULCO's The Canaanite God Rešep (American Oriental Society. Essay No. 8), New Haven/Connecticut 1976: JEA 66, pp. 144-150.

1981

(127) A. EL-SAYED MAHMUD, A New Temple for Hathor at Memphis, Warminster 1978: BiOr 38, col. 299-300.
(128) I. BESTE, Skarabäen (Corpus Antiquitatum Aegyptiacarum, Hannover), Mainz 1978 (Teil 1) und 1979 (Teil 2 und 3): BiOr 38, col. 312-317.

1983

(129) The Scarabs [in:] D. PRICE WILLIAMS, The Tombs of the Middle-Bronze Age II Period from the "500" Cemetery at Tell el-Fara (South), London 1977: BiOr 40, col. 624-625.

1984

(130) M. BIETAK, Avaris and Piramesse. Archaeological Exploration in the Eastern Nile Delta [extrait de: Proceedings of the British Academy 65 (London 1979, éd. 1981) pp. 225-289]: ChdE 59, pp. 74-77.

Scarabs

and other Small Finds

from Recent Excavations in Israel

The Catalogue System Employed

NO.:   continuous numbering; for each site, already published material is mentioned first, followed by as yet unpublished items in the order of their field inventory no.

ITEM:
- form
- for MB scarabs: head, back and side types according to Tufnell, StSc II pp. 31-38
- potential damage: progressively from abraded to battered to damaged; if the item is in good condition, this is not noted
- type of engraving: incised linear, sunk relief, bas relief, etc.
- material, glaze, etc.
- measurements: length, breadth and height in mm.

DECORATION: description of elements on the base followed by any decoration on the back

PARALLELS:
- for MB Scarabs: Design Classes according to Tufnell, StSc II
- pieces with similar motifs or style (for short titles and abbreviations see bibliography of reference works cited at the end of the volume)

DATE: in principle this is based on the scarab only (head, back and side types, decoration, stylistic features, royal names, comparative material, etc.)

PROVENANCE:
- precise location wherever possible: area, locus, stratum with date suggested by the excavators
- field inventory no.

COLLECTION:
- present location of the piece wherever known
- registration number (IDAM, Institute, etc.) wherever known

BIBLIOGRAPHY: preliminary publications where the piece was either routinely mentioned or specifically discussed (for short titles and abbreviations see bibliography of reference works cited at the end of the volume)

N.B.: If not stated otherwise, line drawings in the catalogue are reproduced 3:1, photographs on the plates 2:1.

Tell Abu Zureiq

(isr. Tel Zariq, ca. 1 km. south-east of Kibbutz Ha-Zorea[c]; 1623/2267)

A Note on the Recovery of these Scarabs

During the excavation in Area C at Abu Zureiq (1970-1971; cf. E. Anati, Hazorea: IEJ 21 [1971] pp. 172-173; id., Abu Zureiq [Hazorea]: RB 78 [1971] pp. 582-584), Prof. Anati requested me to complete the excavation of a tomb containing finds of the MB II A and MB II B/C periods.

The entrance of the MB II A tomb was a sloping passage - cut into the surface of the rock from the Northeast - leading into a cave, the interior of which was divided into two parts by a low wall of natural rock. The oval part near the entrance was 2.45 m. below the surface, while the second, crescent-shaped part lay 2.20 m. below the surface.

The surface of the rock around the tomb was honeycombed with bell-shaped silos, about 1.5 to 1.8 m. in depth, dating to the late Iron or Persian periods, represented by concentric circles on the plan, the outer one giving the circumference of the bottom and the inner one the opening of the silo at the surface (loci 507, 508, 517, 518, 523). Silo/locus 507 was cut into the passage of the tomb-entrance, so that a stone wall had to be erected there.

The passage was sealed with plaster after the final burial of the MB II A period. In the MB II B/C period, however, a second entrance was forced into the crescent-formed rear part of the cave, from the West. A third opening was created when the *silo/locus 517* was cut. The floor of this silo was 1.48 m. below the surface, half of it opening into the tomb. The first of these disturbances may account for the mixed nature of the scarabs found within the tomb. The second led to their presence being overlooked when the tomb was plundered. Most of the scarabs were found at the floor level of the tomb, in the intrusive soil and pebbles *below and near locus 517*. It is most probable that this intrusive layer was washed down after the MB II B/C period, preventing the discovery and removal of the scarabs.

Six of seven scarabs found in the tomb came from the *concentration below locus 517*, together with a silver crescent pendant (H 71-378) and a silver ring (H 71-377), which probably served as the setting for a scarab. Three of these scarabs (H 71-372, H 71-373 and H 71-374) had undecorated bases and will not be published here.

A single scarab (H 71-390; below No. 2) was discovered near the remains of a skull on the floor in the southern corner of the crescent-shaped part of the tomb.

Ezra Meyerhof,
Kibbutz Ha-Zorea[c]

19

1   ITEM: Scarab, D3/0/d5, break around hole at lower back; sunk relief, hatching and cross-hatching; steatite (?); 17.8 x 13.2 x 8.4 mm.
DECORATION: Horizontally arranged: a lion, with tail above his back, assaults an ibex or antelope, whose head is turned toward his attacker.
PARALLELS: Design Class 9B, 9E. Petrie, BP I pl. 12:125. Id., BP II pl. 43: 14. Giveon, Scarabs British Museum pp. 118-119 no. 23. Matz, CMS I no. 278.
DATE: Hyksos, Dyn. XV (ca. 1650-1550 B.C.E.).
PROVENANCE: Area C, disturbed tomb, below locus 517; MB II A-B (ca. 1850-1600 B.C.E.).
COLLECTION: Ha-Zorea^c, Wilfried Israel Museum No. H 71-389. IDAM 72-5827.

2   ITEM: Scarab, A1/0/e7, border slightly abraded, schematic linear engraving with scratched hatching; dark grey-green jasper; 18.3 x 12.8 x 9.2 mm.
DECORATION: An open-mouthed human figure with an elaborate headdress stands before two plants, the stalk of the taller in the tight grip of his left hand; the hand of the relaxed right arm is empty; behind him is perhaps an *i*-reed, below which is a short bent line.
PARALLELS: Design Class 10A1b. For style and motif, see the parallels for no. 4 below; for the plants esp. Petrie, AG IV pls. 8 and 9:385 = Rowe, Catalogue no. 74.
DATE: Dyn. XIII-XV (ca. 1750-1550 B.C.E.).
PROVENANCE: Area C, disturbed tomb; MB II A-B (ca. 1850-1600 B.C.E.).
COLLECTION: Ha-Zorea^c, Wilfried Israel Museum No. H 71-376. IDAM 72-5828.

3   ITEM: Scarab, A5/dec./d6, back and head/clypeus damaged, linear engraving; dark grey steatite, white glazed; 20.6 x 14.4 x 8.1 mm.
DECORATION: A lotus flower separates two symmetrical standing human figures with shoulder-length hair and knee-length kilts. Each figure grasps the flower stalk before him with one hand, while the other arm ist relaxed: in the right hand of the left figure is an ^cnh-sign. Two blossoms (papyrus?) are also set at knee-level; below is a *nb*-sign. The back is also decorated, with symmetrical curls on the elytra, and a lotus blossom (?) on the pronotum.
PARALLELS: Design Classes 1E3, 10Bb. Petrie, BP I pl. 39:437. Id., AG IV pls. 5:115 and 7:224. Gamer-Wallert, Iberische Halbinsel no. B 19. Back: Tufnell, Lachish IV pls. 37/38:316 and 32:107.
DATE: Early Hyksos, Dyn. XV (ca. 1650-1600 B.C.E.).
PROVENANCE: Area C, disturbed tomb, below locus 517; MB II A-B/C (ca. 1850-1600 B.C.E.).
COLLECTION: Ha-Zorea^c, Wilfried Israel Museum No. H 71-375. IDAM 72-5828/1.

2:1

2:1

2:1

4   ITEM: Scarab, A1/0/e5, slightly abraded, linear engraving; green jasper; 15.2 x 10.9 x 7.4 mm.

DECORATION: A striding or standing match-stick human figure, open-mouthed and armed (or holding an $^c n\underline{h}$-sign in the relaxed right hand), whose left forearm is raised confronting a series of signs. The headdress is strikingly prominent. A small protuberance at waist level might be related to the slight thickening of the right thigh, revealing a weapon (or its sheath) or a codpiece. Between the head and the arm is a V-shaped sign, followed by three additional signs in front of the figure: an upside-down T-shape (^{c}?), a zig-zag (n?), and an X-shaped sign. Reading $^c n$, "return", disregards the V-shaped sign, or considers it to be a remarkably unsuccessful i-prefix. The same sign appears however in the same position on a parallel (Tufnell, Lachish IV pls. 35/36:237), with the cross representing the walking legs determinative. Alternative readings (as, e.g., $^c n$ "beautiful") are no less improbable. The signs could represent a personal name.

PARALLELS: Design Classes 3C, 10A1f. Similarity in motif or elements: Kenyon, Jericho II fig. 301:10 (PN *idnr*; see Ranke, PN I 54,14). Petrie, Gerar pl. 17:40. Id., AG I pl. 14:113 = Rowe, Catalogue no. 177. Loud, Megiddo II pl. 151:145. Similarity in style: Tufnell, Lachish IV pls. 35/36:237. Grant, Ain Shems II pl. 51:5. Guy, Megiddo Tombs pl. 106:12 = Rowe, Catalogue no. 74. Macalister, Gezer II p. 329 no. 397, III pl. 209:17. Rowe, Catalogue nos. 291 (Shechem) and 361 (Megiddo). Loud, Megiddo II pl. 150:80 and 104; pl. 151: 145. Also to be compared are an unpublished piece in the Dayan Collection and no. 2 above.

DATE: Dyn. XIII-XV (ca. 1750-1550 B.C.E.).

PROVENANCE: Area C, disturbed tomb, below locus 517; MB II A-B (ca. 1850-1600 B.C.E.).

COLLECTION: Ha-Zorea^c, Wilfried Israel Museum, H 71-390. IDAM 72-5830.

Achziv

The first group of Achziv scarabs presented here are those discovered by Dr. M.W. Prausnitz during the three seasons (1958, 1960, 1963) of excavations he directed at Achziv on behalf of the Israel Department of Antiquities and the University of Rome. The site had been previously excavated in the early 1940's, by I. Ben-Dor for the Department of Antiquities. These excavations revealed a settlement pattern developing through the Middle and Late Bronze Ages, with a considerable expansion during the Iron Age. Dr. Prausnitz' excavations concentrated on the three Iron Age cemeteries belonging to the city: the Southern Cemetery of Minet Achziv (or Buqbaq), the Eastern Cemetery of Gesher Achziv (or er-Ras), and another cemetery at the eastern slope of the tell. The variety of designs indicates the cultural interaction typical of scarabs from the Levant. Dr. M.W. Prausnitz has generously consented to the publication of the following scarabs in this volume.

  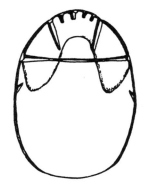

23

5   ITEM: Scarab, edges battered; sunk relief; white steatite, traces of yellow glaze; 16 x 10.6 x 7.7 mm.
DECORATION: Inscription: *Ḫnsw m s3* <.*y*> "Khonsu (the Theban moon-god) is <my> protection".
PARALLELS: This is precisely the kind of amuletic interpretation that one would expect a scarab to carry. It is thus very well represented in the collections. Parallels include: Petrie, BDS pl. 12:698. Hornung/Staehelin, Skarabäen Basel nos. MV 12 and Va 9. Vercoutter, Les Objets egytiens nos. 386-387. Gjerstad, Swedish Cyprus Expedition II p. 840 no. 2421 = pl. 247:1. Ward, PSBA 22 (1900) pl. 8:316. Dunbabin, Perachora II fig. 31:161. Giveon, Scarabs British Museum pp. 182-183 no. 15. Sliwa, Cracow pl. 17:96. Jaeger, Scarabées Menkhéperrê p. 69 § 286.
DATE: Dyn. XXVI (664-525 B.C.E.).
PROVENANCE: Minet Achziv, Southern Cemetery, locus/tomb 24, cremation burial; Late Iron Age II C (ca. 650-550 B.C.E.). Field no. 24/10.
COLLECTION: Jerusalem, IDAM 58-622.

6   ITEM: Scarab, the periphery of the longitudinal hole slightly abraded at each end, rim damaged; sunk relief; white steatite, remains of ochre glaze; 14.25 x 10.7 x 6.9 mm.
DECORATION: Horizontally arranged: an ichneumon with head uplifted below a solar disk and a *iwn*-column (see below no. 17 [Achziv]). Before resorting to a cryptographic reading as "Amun" (Hornung/Staehelin, Skarabäen Basel p. 176) one might reflect on the meaning of the scarab as such, and thus (1) take account of an "ichneumon of Re^C" (or an ichneumon as the "image of Re^C", cf. Daressy, ASAE 18 [1918] p. 132); (2) the fact that the *iwn*-column is used to write Heliopolis, Re^C's own city, and (3) Atum's occasional identity as an ichneumon (Sethe, ZÄS 63 [1928] pp. 50-53) could indicate that the design should be interpreted as "Re^C-Atum of Heliopolis" or something similar.
PARALLELS: No. 17 below (Achziv). Petrie, Tanis I pl. 12:2. Id., Tanis II pl. 8:47 and 48. Id., SCN pl. 54:25.L.9. Gjerstad, Swedish Cyprus Expedition II pl. 246:2252. Matouk, Corpus II p. 389 nos. 844-849. Petrie, BP I pl. 48:568. Hornung/Staehelin, Skarabäen Basel nos. 47 and 573 (with literature for the variations with the *m3^Ct*-feather in place of the *iwn*-column which could also be read als "*M3^Ct* of Re^C-Atum" or similarly. The goddess *M3^Ct* was considered to be the daughter of Re^C. Hornung/Staehelin assume that both variations represented cryptographic writings of the name "Amun". Another alternative would be to read these as *Nb-m3^Ct-R^C*, where the ichneumon would assume the phonetic value *n*, as according to the hypothetical cryptographic reading. This is however improbable in this epoch.) See also Brunner-Traut, Spitzmaus und Ichneumon, *passim*.
DATE: Dyn. XXVI (664-525).
PROVENANCE: Minet Achziv, Southern Cemetery, locus/tomb 24, cremation burial; Late Iron Age II C (650-550). Field no. 24/58.
COLLECTION: Jerusalem, IDAM 58-629.

 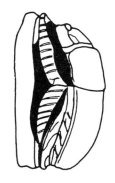 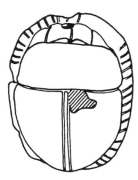

7   ITEM: Scarab, linear engraving, hatching (?); white steatite; 11 x 8 x 5 mm.
DECORATION: A *nfr*-sign is situated between two S-spiral ornaments above and below it, while flanked by two rather unconventional signs which may derivate from stylized winged sun-disks with uraei.
PARALLELS: Giveon/Kertesz, Acco nos. 14-15. Kition no. 1037 (600-450 B.C.E.). Hall, Catalogue no. 2180. Newberry, CG pl. 4:36190.
DATE: End of Dyn. XIX - beginning of Dyn. XXII (ca. 1200-900 B.C.E.).
PROVENANCE: Minet Achziv, Southern Cemetery, inside the chamber of tomb 606; Iron Age I - II A (1150-900 B.C.E.). Field no. 606/107.
COLLECTION: Jerusalem, IDAM.

8   ITEM: Scarab, apparently broken and glued; partly linear engraving, partly sunk relief with hatching; white steatite; 16 x 11.7 x 7.4 mm.
DECORATION: Two interlocking S-spirals flanked by two symmetrical "chains"; each of these is composed of two tear-drop figures, separated from each other by small disks, with two others ornamenting the pointed distal ends of each.
PARALLELS: Petrie, AG IV pl. 5:114. Gjerstad, Swedish Cyprus Expedition III p. 598 and pl. 204:23c.
DATE: End of Dyn. XIX - beginning of Dyn. XXII (ca. 1200-900 B.C.E.).
PROVENANCE: Minet Achziv, Southern Cemetery, inside the chamber of tomb 606; Iron Age I - II A (1150-900 B.C.E.). Field No. 606/108.
COLLECTION: Jerusalem, IDAM (?).

9   ITEM: Scarab, right side of head partially damaged; sunk relief, cross strokes; yellow-white steatite, on a silver ring, to which a tube segment has been soldered; this may have been intended for suspension on a string; 15.7 x 11.3 x 7.8 mm.
DECORATION: Within a single-line border, i.e. not a cartouche: two leopard heads, below two solar disks, and above a *nb*-sign. Although one of the solar disks would thus be rendered superfluous, it does not seem inappropriate to read the name Nb-$p\d{h}tj$-R^c, i.e. Ahmose I (1540-1525 B.C.E.), the founder of Dyn. XVIII.
PARALLELS: Hornung/Staehelin, Skarabäen Basel p. 56, fig. 7. Jaeger, Scarabées Menkhéperrê pp. 137.254.255.
DATE: Dyn. XVIII (ca. 1540-1295 B.C.E.).
PROVENANCE: Minet Achziv, Southern Cemetery, inside the chamber of tomb 606; Iron Age I - II A (1150-900 B.C.E.).
COLLECTION: Jerusalem, IDAM 58-624.

10   ITEM: Scarab, sunk relief and linear engraving, hatching; white steatite; 13.9 x 9.5 x 6.3 mm.
DECORATION: A double cross pattern with a crossed spiral woven into a rosette. Above and below are *nwb*-signs.

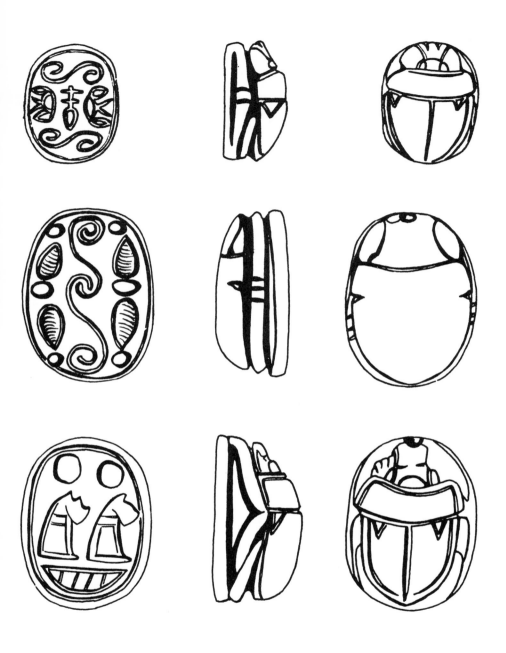

PARALLELS: Design Class 5. Petrie, BP I pls. 12:168 and 43:502. Newberry, Timins Collection pl. 17:35.
DATE: End of Dyn. XIX - Dyn. XX (ca. 1200-1075 B.C.E.).
PROVENANCE: Cemetery on the eastern slope of the tell, cist tomb 1009; Iron Age I (1150-1000 B.C.E.). Field no. 1009/28 (resp. 1009/6324).
COLLECTION: Rome, Istituto del Vicino Oriente.

11   ITEM: Scarab, rim damaged; sunk relief, some scratched hatching; carnelian; 11.8 x 8.9 x 6.3 mm.
DECORATION: Horizontally divided into two registers. The upper register contains a *nb*-sign, below which are the walking legs, with a *t* and a *p*-shaped sign, as well as a second *t* or a second *nb*. In the lower register one can read *ip*, with an enigmatic sign behind it. The upper half could read *nmt.t nb.t* "(My) every stride" (on the assumption that the *p* is actually a thickened determinative stroke). The horizontal line may be read as *n*. In several parallels the lower register refers to Karnak (*ip.t sw.t*) or Amun, the whole meaning "My every stride belongs to Amun/Karnak", according to Drioton, Pages d'Egyptologie p. 126 no. 3. This item shows only *ip.t* in the lower register, the whole thus meaning "(My) every stride belongs to the harem (of Amun, i.e. Luxor)". No border line.
In the upper register the *p*-shaped stroke is somewhat disconcerting, when compared to the *p* in the lower register. It is remarkable that such an inept inscription was engraved in such a valuable material and it is not insignificant that carnelian was in fact almost never etched in Egypt. This is most probably an imitation inscription on an anepigraphic scarab exported from Egypt.
PARALLELS: Giveon, Scarabs British Museum pp. 166-167 no. 2. Hornung/ Staehelin, Skarabäen Basel no. 749. Newberry, Scarabs pl. 39:2-3. Id., Timins Collection pl. 12:5-6. Petrie, Gerar pl. 17:29. Cf. Jaeger, Scarabées Menkhéper-rê p. 65 § 264.
DATE: Iron Age I - II A (1150-900 B.C. E.), although the scarab itself may date to an earlier period.
PROVENANCE: Cemetery on the eastern slope of the tell, cist tomb 1009; Iron Age I (1150-1000 B.C.E.). Field No. 1009/31.
COLLECTION: Jerusalem, IDAM.

12   ITEM: Scarab, linear engraving; white steatite; 12.5 x 9 x 5.5 mm.
DECORATION: A human figure, clad in a short kilt and a tight fitting shirt, whose arms hang relaxed at his sides, is shown with the head in profile, but the torso (at least) in front view, flanked by schematic signs, with another between his legs. The headdress (with horned helmet?) might be taken to resemble the one characteristic of the Philistines or the "Peoples of the Sea" as shown in the reliefs at Medinet Habu. However, the decoration might equally represent Onuris, who has four vertical feathers in his headdress. The appendage on the chin is probably intended to be a short beard. It is possible that the objects depicted on the left are an (unstrung?) composite bow and a curved *ḫpš*-sword. The object

 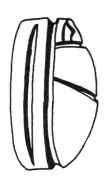 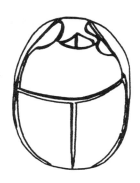

between the warrior's legs could be an uraeus, while the sign on the right defies interpretation.
PARALLELS: For the Philistine headdress see Galling, Ugaritica VI pp. 247-265, and Schachermeyr, ibid. pp. 451-459. The back shows a certain affinity to Petrie, SCN no. 19.2.35, pl. 39:35 = pl. 70:83. Cf. Jaeger, Scarabées Menkhéperrê, pp. 185-187.
DATE: Dyn. XIX-XX (ca. 1295-1070 B.C.E.).
PROVENANCE: Cemetery on the eastern slope of the tell, cist tomb; Iron Age I (1150-1000 B.C.E.). Field no. X/1963.
COLLECTION: Jerusalem, IDAM.

13   ITEM: Scaraboid, severely abraded; sunk relief; yellow steatite, traces of white glaze; 14.8 x 10.9 x 5.8 mm.
DECORATION: A almond-like design within which are three pointed ovals divides the design horizontally into two essentially symmetrical halves. Above and below are vertical mace-like figures framed by parallel lines, with three parallel lines perpendicular to each of these latter lines in the remaining spaces on the sides.
PARALLELS: Hölbl (SAK 7 [1979] p. 102 n. 38; id., Altitalien II p. 184 no. 764) traces the origin of this device back to Mn-hpr-R^c in an oval flanked by $wd3t$-eyes (cf. Starkey/Harding, BP II pl. 73:37. Matthiae Scandone, Scarabei di Cagliari no. I 1 = Hölbl, Sardinien I p. 177; II pl. 103:1. Vercoutter, Objets égyptiens no. 319).
DATE: Dyn. XX (1190-1075 B.C.E.).
PROVENANCE: Gesher Achziv (er-Ras), Eastern Cemetery, tomb 4012; end of Iron Age I - end of Iron Age II (ca. 1050-650 B.C.E.). Field no. 4012/17A (resp. 4012/631).
COLLECTION: Jerusalem, IDAM.

14   ITEM: Fragment of a plaque (?); sunk relief; 8 x 5 x 2 mm.
DECORATION: Assyrian-type winged disk (?) with appendages; cf. Mayer-Opficius, UF 16 (1984) pp. 189-236. Despite the fragmentary state of preservation of this piece, the form and arrangement of the feathers does make it reasonably clear that the protruding rectangle and the linear appendages should not be interpreted as tail feathers and legs nor the vertical line as neck. An interpretation of the decoration as Nekhbet (cf. Matouk, Corpus II p. 347 nos. 391-392) has to be excluded for the same reason. No border line visible.
DATE: First half of 1st millennium B.C.E.
PROVENANCE: Gesher Achziv (er-Ras), Eastern Cemetery, tomb 4012; end of Iron Age I - end of Iron Age II (ca. 1050-650 B.C.E.). Field no. 4012/17B.
COLLECTION: Rome, Istituto del Vicino Oriente.

15   ITEM: Scarab; shallow sunk relief; yellow steatite; 8.3 x 6.1 x 4.1 mm.
DECORATION: Horizontally arranged: the sign hs, the goddess $M3^ct$ (with an ^cnh on her lap) and the scholar disk R^c, meaning perhaps, "Praised is the $M3^ct$

of Re^c". The emphasis on $M3^c t$ and the solar deity is frequent on scarabs, as the goddess $M3^c t$ was regarded as being the daughter of the Sun-God Re^c.
PARALLELS: The location of the solar disk (R^c) at the end remains somewhat remarkable, but not without a parallel: Hornung/Staehelin, Skarabäen Basel nos. 407 and B 19. Vodoz, Genève no. 63.
DATE: Dyn. XVIII (ca. 1540-1295 B.C.E.) or Dyn. XXV-XXVI (ca. 780-525 B.C.E.).
PROVENANCE: Gesher Achziv (er-Ras), Eastern Cemetery, tomb 4012; end of Iron Age I - end of Iron Age II C (ca. 1050-650 B.C.E.). Field no. 4012/17C.
COLLECTION: Jerusalem, IDAM.

16   ITEM: Scarab, battered, head and base partly damaged; broad linear engraving, crude; steatite (?); 18.3 x 14 x 9.1 mm.
DECORATION: Horizontally arranged: a centrally placed stylized "sacred tree" flanked by two quadrupeds, doubtless simplified winged griffins, each of them touching the tree with the mouth and a single outstretched paw. The parallels show a remarkable development with rather inept forms - derived from Mycenaen parallels? - in the second half of LB II but fine versions well dated to the early Iron Age, indicating that this particular type experienced an artistic revival rather than a degradation in the course of the early Iron Age.
PARALLELS: Murray, Excavations in Cyprus pp. 99-100 and fig. 147:41. Vollenweider, Genève no. 181. Wainwright, Balabish pl. 24:20. Loud, Megiddo I pl. 67:45 (middle register). This is a typical motif in Cypriote and Phoenician art of the early Iron Age: cf., e.g., Markoe, Bowls nos. Cy 1, 4 and 8.
DATE: Middle of Iron Age II C (ca. 750-650 B.C.E.).
PROVENANCE: Gesher Achziv (er-Ras), Eastern Cemetery, tomb 4012; end of Iron Age I - end of Iron Age II C (1050-650 B.C.E.).
COLLECTION: Jerusalem, IDAM 63-950.

17   ITEM: Scarab, part of the head broken, base rim slightly battered; sunk relief; paste (?); 11.9 x 8.6 x 5.5 mm.
DECORATION: Horizontally arranged: an ichneumon beneath a solar disk (R^c) and a *iwn*-column, meaning "Re^c-Atum of Heliopolis", or "Amun", cryptographically written.
PARALLELS: See above no. 6 (Achziv).
DATE: Dyn. XXVI (664-525 B.C.E.).
PROVENANCE: Minet Achziv, Southern Cemetery; exact provenance not specified.
COLLECTION: Jerusalem, IDAM.

18   ITEM: Seal impression, fragmentary; clay; 10 x *6.3 mm.
DECORATION: The prenomen Wsr-$m3^c t$(?)-R^c and the usual epithet stp-$<n>$-R^c of Ramesses II (1279-1213 B.C.E.); the feather on the goddess's head seems to be missing.
PARALLELS: Petrie, SCN pl. 41:19.3.56-59.

2:1

DATE: Probably Dyn. XIX, reign of Ramesses II (1279-1213 B.C.E.).
PROVENANCE: Achziv (?).
COLLECTION: Jerusalem, IDAM.

The following scarabs are also apparently from Achziv, but not from excavated material. No. 19 was found in 1959 by Mr. Moshe Duḥovni of Kibbutz Ḥanita on the surface of the coast in the neighbourhood of Achziv. The others form a part of the private collection of Mr. Justus Meyer of Nahariya, who has generously placed them at our disposal.

19 ITEM: Scarab, faint traces of prothorax and wing-cases visible, head and clypeus indicated, legs deeply cut open; sunk relief with hatching and cross hatching; white bone, traces of white glaze on the back, copper oxide visible on the top hole; 16 x 11.5 x 7 mm.
DECORATION: A sphinx whose human head is adorned with Pharaoh's double crown rears with its pair of double wings spread and its forepaws before it. It would appear to be wearing an elaborate pectoral or, more likely, a scaled corselet mail tunic. The pedestal upon which it stands is a *nb*-sign. Between its raised tail and a wing is a strange sign, like a *mn* or an *n*. A solar disk above a *mn* (or both signs to be taken as *3ḫt*?) would appear to flank each side of the crown, above which might be a *šn*-ring.
PARALLELS: Hornung/Staehelin, Skarabäen Basel no. B 24. Vollenweider, Genève no. 159. Two cases of *sḫm*-signs with solar disks are to be found in Vodoz, Genève nos. 61 and D 443. It is possible that the horizon-sign *3ḫt* lies behind this.
DATE: Dyn. XX - mid-Dyn. XXII (ca. 1150-800 B.C.E.).
PROVENANCE: Found on the surface of the coast in the neighbourhood of Achziv.
COLLECTION:

20 ITEM: Scarab, base slightly damaged on upper left side; sunk relief, hatching; steatite; ca. 14 x 10 x 6 mm.
DECORATION: An unidentifiable creature but probably a deformed falcon, whose spread wings protect the name *Mn-ḫpr-Rᶜ*, prenomen of Tuthmosis III (1479-1426 B.C.E.), enclosed within a cartouche; above this an ᶜ3-pillar, alongside which a *nṯr*-sign, turned upside down, is probably to be understood, meaning "the great god". Below there is a *nb*-sign.
PARALLELS: Cf. Jaeger, Scarabées Menkhéperrê pp. 159-160. Bruyère, Deir el-Médineh 15, p. 70, fig. 34:f. 5 (= Jaeger, op. cit. pp. 125 ill. 306 and 160 ill. 451). Hayes, Scepter of Egypt II p. 77 fig. 41 (upper left). Petrie, SCN pl. 53: 25.C.10. Vodoz, Genève no. 22.
DATE: Dyn. XIX-XX (1292-1075 B.C.E.) or later.
PROVENANCE: Achziv (?).
COLLECTION: Nahariya, Justus Meyer.

34

21   ITEM: Scarab; sunk relief, hatching and cross hatching; steatite; 14.8 x 11 x 6.5 mm.
DECORATION: Horizontally arranged: a lying bearded sphinx with a blue crown with uraeus, beneath a protective winged uraeus. Before the sphinx is a *nṯr*-sign.
PARALLELS: With double crown and *M3ᶜt* in front: Giveon, Scarabs British Museum, pp. 32-35 nos. 34-35, pp. 42-43 nos. 61-62; with ᶜnḫ in front: ibid., pp. 172-173 no. 4.
DATE: Dyn. XIX-XX (ca. 1292-1075 B.C.E.).
PROVENANCE: Achziv (?).
COLLECTION: Nahariya, Justus Meyer.

22   ITEM: Scarab, rim damaged; sunk relief; steatite; 16 x 11 x 6 mm.
DECORATION: The Egyptian god Bes with feather-crown and lion-tail, holding two prisoners. Below them is a *nb*-sign; flanking the feather-crown are two a-morphous shapes, perhaps more prisoners.
PARALLELS: Jaeger, Scarabées Menkhéperrê p. 214 §§ 1399-1402.
DATE: Dyn. XIX-XX (ca. 1292-1075 B.C.E.).
PROVENANCE: Achziv (?).
COLLECTION: Nahariya, Justus Meyer.

23   ITEM: Scarab, sunk relief; steatite; 11 x 8 x 4,5 mm.
DECORATION: A standing or striding, probably falcon-headed anthropoid figure whose relaxed arms are extended at his sides; in front of him an undistinguished shape, probably a badly drawn *i*-reed. No border line.
PARALLELS: Petrie, BP I pls. 31:315; 33:364; 35:392; 43:504 and 532.
DATE: Dyn. XIX-XX (ca. 1292-1075 B.C.E.).
PROVENANCE: Achziv (?).
COLLECTION: Nahariya, Justus Meyer.

24   ITEM: Scarab, slightly damaged at top of base; sunk relief; steatite; 12.5 x 9 x 6 mm.
DECORATION: A *nfr*-sign between two *m3ᶜt*-feathers, with a *nb*-sign below. A cryptographic writing of the divine name *Imn* "Amun" may be intended (cf. Jaeger, Scarabées Menkhéperrê p. 294 n. 218).
PARALLELS: Petrie, BP I pl. 40:473. Id., Naukratis I pl. 37:109. Hölbl, Sardinien II pls. 124:3 and 132:1.
DATE: Dyn. XXVI (664-525 B.C.E.).
PROVENANCE: Achziv (?).
COLLECTION: Nahariya, Justus Meyer.

25   ITEM: Scarab, edges slightly battered; sunk relief, scratched hatching; steatite; 17 x 12.6 x 6.5 mm.
DECORATION: Below a creature which could be a donkey with the head and squared ears of the Seth-animal, with whom the former was frequently identified.

While this creature was clearly meant to be depicted in motion, the execution was not equal to the task, with the result that the legs shown would have been insufficient for balance, let alone movement. Above are a Red Crown, an owl (*m*) and two horizontal strokes beneath the owl (perhaps intended to signify "the two lands"?). The upper signs could make reference to Amun (cf. Hornung/ Staehelin, Skarabäen Basel no. 749).
DATE: Probably Dyn. XXII-XXV (ca. 944-656 B.C.E.).
PROVENANCE: Achziv (?).
COLLECTION: Nahariya, Justus Meyer.

26   ITEM: Scarab, battered; sunk relief; steatite; 16 x 12 x 6 mm.
DECORATION: On the left: a solar disk (*R^c*) above a *mn*, and *nṯr ^{c}nḫ* ("the living god"). On the right is probably a badly executed falcon turned right and wearing a Red Crown. The base is formed by a *nb*-sign.
DATE: Probably Dyn. XXII-XXV (ca. 944-656 B.C.E.).
PROVENANCE: Achziv (?).
COLLECTION: Nahariya, Justus Meyer.

27   ITEM: Scarab, damaged; linear engraving, hatching; steatite; *13.5 x 10 x 7.9 mm.
DECORATION: A diphylous rosette divides the base into two symmetrical halves, each consisting of an S-spiral flanked by two irregular shapes, as of two tear drops still united.
DATE: End of Dyn. XIX - beginning of Dyn. XXII (ca. 1200-900 B.C.E.).
PROVENANCE: Achziv (?).
COLLECTION: Nahariya, Justus Meyer.

28   ITEM: A seal in the form of a lion couchant, base severely abraded; sunk relief; fayence; 14 x 10 x 9 mm.
DECORATION: A striding lion before whom is a single stroke, probably derived from an *i*-reed. No border line.
PARALLELS: Lamon/Shipton, Megiddo I pl. 69:59. Below nos. 69 and 74 (Jerishe).
DATE: End of Dyn. XIX - beginning of Dyn. XXII (ca. 1200-900 B.C.E.).
PROVENANCE: Achziv (?).
COLLECTION: Nahariya, Justus Meyer.

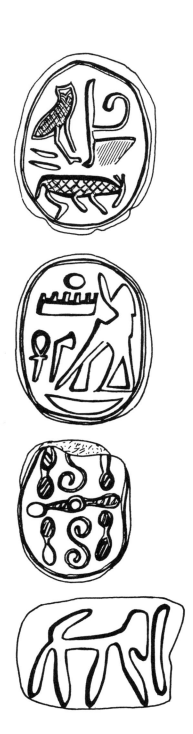

Tel Aphek

W. F. Albright's survey (1923) and the excavations conducted by J. Ory in 1935-36 established that the stratigraphy of Tel Aphek (arabic Ras el-ᶜAin) reached from the early third millennium into the first. Prof. M. Kochavi of the Institute of Archaeology, Tel Aviv University, started a new excavation at the site in the 1970's, which lead to the discovery of a palace of MB I date and confirmed that the tell was a significant centre throughout the second millennium B.C.E. The quality and variety of the scarabs which we are able to present here thanks to the generosity of Prof. Kochavi can only reinforce this point, giving a representative selection of designs typical of the various periods of the second millennium.

29   ITEM: Scarab, B6/0/d8, rim and one side damaged; linear engraving; steatite; 13 x 8 x 5 mm.
DECORATION: Within a border of oblong interlocking spirals: anra-type group of hieroglyphic signs ($ḫ^c$, a figure-eight loop, *mn*, ^{c} and *n*). The group is without any apparent meaning.
PARALLELS: Design Classes 3C, 7A2a. Petrie, BP I pl. 7:51-52. Tufnell, Lachish IV pl. 30/31:23.
DATE: Dyn. XIII-XV (ca. 1750-1550 B.C.E.).
PROVENANCE: Area G, built tomb, locus 1200; LB II B (1300-1150 B.C.E.). Field no. 12039/80.
COLLECTION: On exposition in the Petaḥ Tiqvah Museum.
BIBLIOGRAPHY: Kochavi, Aphek-Antipatris, unnumbered plate (p. 29/20).

30   ITEM: Scarab, B4?/0/e10; linear engraving, partially hatched; steatite; 16 x 11 x 7 mm.
DECORATION: Horizontally arranged: a striding ibex, with two space-filling elements: in front a debased uraeus turned upward, behind the horns another uraeus turned outward.
PARALLELS: Design Class 9B. Petrie, AG I pl. 14:86. Id., BP I pl. 12:144. Id., Hyksos and Israelite Cities pl. 6:5. Id., AG V pl. 10:116-118 and pl. 42. Giveon, Scarabs British Museum pp. 56-57 no. 1 and pp. 84-85 no. 70. Hornung/Staehelin, Skarabäen Basel nos. B 52 and D 22.
DATE: Dyn. XIII-XV (ca. 1750-1550 B.C.E.) or later.
PROVENANCE: Area G, built tomb, locus 1200; LB II B (1300-1150 B.C.E.). Field no. 12058/80.
COLLECTION: Tel Aviv University, Institute of Archaeology (M. Kochavi).
BIBLIOGRAPHY: Kochavi, Aphek-Antipatris, unnumbered plate (p. 29/20).

31   ITEM: Scarab; sunk relief, very deep, partially hatched; steatite; 18 x 13 x 4 mm.
DECORATION: An anthropomorphic falcon headed figure with a solar disk above its head (probably the Sun-god, Re^c-Harakhte) extends the left hand, holding a w3s-sceptre, before which is a m3^{c}t-feather. Beneath this scene is a nb-sign.
PARALLELS: Matouk, Corpus II p. 376:155. Petrie, Hyksos and Israelite Cities pl. 11:228. Id., BP I pl. 43:504 and 532. Giveon, Scarabs British Museum pp. 46-47 no. 69.
DATE: Dyn. XIX - early Dyn. XX (ca. 1292-1150 B.C.E.).
PROVENANCE: Area G, built tomb, locus 1200; LB II B (1300-1150 B.C.E.). Field no. 12066/80.
COLLECTION: Petaḥ Tiqvah Museum.
BIBLIOGRAPHY: Kochavi, Aphek-Antipatris, unnumbered plate (p. 29/20).

32   ITEM: Scarab, D5/0/?, rim slightly damaged; linear engraving; steatite; 22 x 16.5 x   mm.
DECORATION: A convoluted crossed coiled pattern, with two cross bars above and below.
PARALLELS: Design Class 6B2a. Kenyon, Jericho II fig. 290:12.
DATE: Dyn. XII-XV (ca. 1950-1550 B.C.E.).
PROVENANCE: Area D, locus 2503, level 8.30; late Roman (2nd-3rd cent. C.E.). Field no. 25022/70.
COLLECTION: Unknown; illicitly removed from the Petaḥ Tiqvah Museum.
BIBLIOGRAPHY: Giveon, BSFE 81 (1978) pp. 7-8, fig. 2 (not from Lachish!).

33   ITEM: Scarab, D9/0/?; linear engraving; steatite; 18 x 12.5 x   mm.
DECORATION: Within a rope border, three separate, axially aligned and tangentially touching concentric cirles; flanked by an i-reed, and (probably) a twig.
PARALLELS: Design Classes 4E2, 7, 8A.
DATE: Hyksos, Dyn. XV (ca. 1650-1550 B.C.E.).
PROVENANCE: Area D, locus 716, pit with mixed material; MB to Iron Age (2000-587 B.C.E.). Field no. 7148/70.
COLLECTION: Unknown; illicitly removed from the Petaḥ Tiqvah Museum.
BIBLIOGRAPHY: Giveon, BSFE 81 (1978) pp. 7-8, fig. 3 (not from Lachish!).

34   ITEM: Scarab, A4/0/?; linear engraving; steatite; 17 x 12 x   mm.
DECORATION: An involved design with short C-spiral units arranged parallel and perpendicular to one another, providing the illusion of a peltate pattern.
PARALLELS: Design Class 2B2. Kenyon, Jericho II fig. 291:3. Petrie, AG IV pl. 7:228. Rowe, Catalogue no. 192 (Jericho). Newberry, Timins Collection pl. 18:28.
DATE: Dyn. XII-XIII (ca. 1950-1650 B.C.E.).
PROVENANCE: Area X, locus 2731, stratum X-12; LB II B (1300-1150 B.C.E.). Field no. 27598/70.

2:1

  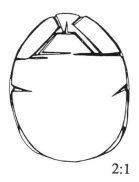

2:1

2:1

2:1

43

COLLECTION: Unknown; illicitly removed from the Petaḥ Tiqvah Museum.
BIBLIOGRAPHY: Giveon, BSFE 81 (1978) pp. 7-8, fig. 4 (not from Lachish!).

35   ITEM: Scarab with metal ring, D6/0/?; linear engraving, partially hatched; steatite; 20 x 14.3 x   mm.
DECORATION: A floral pattern with crossed scrolls leaving a diphylous rosette and two separate symmetrical petals (l./r.), above which is a papyrus plant with three blossoms.
PARALLELS: Design Classes 5 and 1E3.
DATE: Dyn. XIII-XV (ca. 1750-1550 B.C.E.).
PROVENANCE: Area D, locus 703, level 6.68 (surface find). Field no. 7031/70.
COLLECTION: Unknown; illicitly removed from the Petaḥ Tiqvah Museum.
BIBLIOGRAPHY: Giveon, BSFE 81 (1978) pp. 7 and 9, fig. 5 (not from Lachish!).

36   ITEM: Scarab with bronze ring, D5/dec./?; linear engraving; steatite (?); 27 x 20 x   mm.
DECORATION: A central pillar with base, capital and cross bar, between two symmetrical rows of each four concentric circles; each two central circles adjacent to the cross bar are united by arches. The back is decorated with a simple lotus flower on a curved, twig-like stalk.
PARALLELS: Design Class 4B2. Kenyon, Jericho I fig. 285:4. Back: Tufnell, Lachish IV pl. 32:122.
DATE: Dyn. XII-XIII (ca. 1950-1650 B.C.E.).
PROVENANCE: Area A, locus 2105 (pit with mixed material), level 11.15, stratum A-9/10; MB II to LB (1750-1150 B.C.E.). Field no. 2115/80.
COLLECTION: Unknown; illicitly removed from the Petaḥ Tiqvah Museum.
BIBLIOGRAPHY: Giveon, BSFE 81 (1978) pp. 7 and 9, fig. 6 (not from Lachish!).

37   ITEM: Scarab, D1/?/d9, longitudinally fractured, half lost; linear engraving; steatite; 22 x *8 x 10 mm.
DECORATION: One half of an inscription with title and name is preserved: im[y-r] pr ("steward") is clear. Below this is a man beside a partially preserved sign, beneath which stand an n and a r-sign. One suggestion is that the name should be read Nr-[ib] (cf. Ranke, PN I 206,19).
PARALLELS: Design Class 11C.
DATE: Dyn. XII (ca. 1950-1750).
PROVENANCE: Area A, locus 2130, stratum A-13; MB II A (ca. 2000-1750 B.C.E.). Field no. 21252/70.
COLLECTION: Tel Aviv University, Institute of Archaeology (M. Kochavi).
BIBLIOGRAPHY: Giveon, BSFE 81 (1978) pp. 15-16, fig. 13.

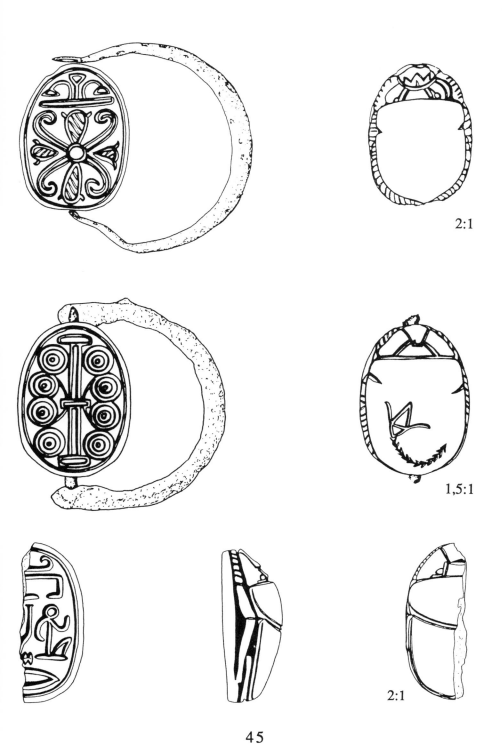

2:1

1,5:1

2:1

45

38 ITEM: Scarab, A5/II/d5; linear engraving, fine, with hatching; steatite (?), glazed white; 13.7 x 10 x 6 mm.
DECORATION: Horizontally arranged: Two ibexes couchant, tête-bêche, form the central composition; they are flanked by two additional tête-bêche creatures, the identity of which is uncertain (perhaps open-mouthed hippopotami). The ibex-horns are inverted. The design is typical of those expected in the early years of scarab manufacture, when tête-bêche and geometric motifs were common. Scarabs of this period are not however particularly numerous.
PARALLELS: Design Class 9B. Giveon, Scarabs British Museum pp. 118-119 no. 25.
DATE: Dyn. XII (ca. 1950-1750 B.C.E.).
PROVENANCE: Area A, locus 547, level 10.50, stratum A-14; MB II A (2000-1750 B.C.E.). Field no. 4769/80.
COLLECTION: Tel Aviv University, Institute of Archaeology (M. Kochavi).
BIBLIOGRAPHY: Giveon, BSFE 81 (1978) pp. 15-16, fig. 14.

39 ITEM: Two impressions of an oval seal with linear engraving; clay; 18 x 12 mm.
DECORATION: A rounded bar (reminiscent of the $t3$-sign) divides the seal horizontally into two registers: above, a Red Crown on a nb is flanked by two $ḥm$; below, a $ḏd$, also on a nb, is flanked by two nfr.
PARALLELS: Design Class 3. Tufnell, Lachish IV pl. 37/38:252.
DATE: Dyn. XII (ca. 1950-1750 B.C.E.).
PROVENANCE: Area A, locus 1355 (fill with mixed material), stratum A-8; MB to Iron Age (2000-587 B.C.E.). Field no. 11064/1.
COLLECTION: Tel Aviv University, Institute of Archaeology (M. Kochavi).
BIBLIOGRAPHY: Giveon, BSFE 81 (1978) pp. 15-16, fig. 15.

40 ITEM: Scarab; partially linear engraving, partially sunk relief; material unknown; 17 x 12.5 x   mm.
DECORATION: The name R^c-mss, nomen of the Ramesside Pharaohs of Dyn. XIX and XX, flanked by two $m3^ct$-feathers. The name is not enclosed in a cartouche.
PARALLELS: Hall, Catalogue no. 2438. Petrie, BP II pl. 50:90 and 105. Cf. id., SCN pl. 38:19.1.8. Hornung/Staehelin, Skarabäen Basel nos. 276.397.B 71. It is curious that Jaeger, Scarabées Menkhéperrê, does not specifically deal with paired "plumes d'autruche" or "plumes de maât". His examples (ills. 166.180. 214.236.243.270.286.310.318.322.343.364.368.376.477.590.594.656) show that this arrangement is primarily typical of Dyn. XVIII with only some rare examples of later date. Our piece confirms the chronological setting in Dyn. XVIII and early XIX.
DATE: Early Dyn. XIX, first half of 13th century B.C.E. The fact that the usual Ramesside epithets (as, e.g., stp-n-R^c, mry-Imn, $ḥq3$-$Iwnw$) are not present indicates that it belongs either to the reign of Ramesses I (1295-1293 B.C.E.) or

46

- less probably - to the early years of his grandson, Ramesses II (1279-1213 B.C.E.).
PROVENANCE: Area X, locus 4018 (pit), level 5.51, stratum X-10; Iron Age I (ca. 1150-1000). Field no. 39284/60.
COLLECTION: Unknown; illicitly removed from the Petaḥ Tiqvah Museum.
BIBLIOGRAPHY: Giveon, BSFE 81 (1978) pp. 15-16, fig. 16a-b.

41   ITEM: Scarab, B4/0/e6; linear engraving; steatite, glazed white; 15.4 x 11.8 x 7 mm.
DECORATION: Four horizontal w3ḏ (signifying freshness or a flourishing condition, in this case representing a wish) between two symmetrically arranged decorative groups consisting of three concentric circles joined by arches.
PARALLELS: Design Class 4B2. Tufnell, Lachish IV pl. 30/31:10.
DATE: Dyn. XII - early Dyn. XIII (ca. 1950-1750 B.C.E.).
PROVENANCE: Area A, locus 74 (non-stratified pit with mixed material), level 14.18; MB - LB (2000-1150 B.C.E.). Field no. 360/1.
COLLECTION: Tel Aviv University, Institute of Archaeology (M. Kochavi).

42   ITEM: Scarab, C7/0/d5, part of border damaged; sunk relief, deep, cross hatching; steatite (?), glazed white; 22.4 x 15.8 x 9.2 mm.
DECORATION: Horizontally arranged: a male human, falconheaded figure in profile, kneeling above a crocodile and between two uraei turned inward; the figure is clad in a tight kilt and holding a bent w3s-scepter.
PARALLELS: Design Classes 9C, 9D, 10C1b. Kenyon, Jericho II figs. 288:15 and 299:25. Vodoz, Genève nos. 36-37. Hornung/Staehelin, Skarabäen Basel no. 897.
DATE: Hyksos, Dyn. XV (ca. 1650-1550 B.C.E.).
PROVENANCE: Area D, locus 2500, level 10.85; late Roman (2nd-3rd cent. C.E.). Field no. 2500/70.
COLLECTION: Tel Aviv University, Institute of Archaeology (M. Kochavi).

43   ITEM: Scarab, D3/0/e9, border slightly damaged; linear engraving, firm; steatite (?), glazed white; 17.5 x 12 x 7.5 mm.
DECORATION: Horizontally arranged: the symbols for nsw bity, "King of Upper and Lower Egypt", stand above a nwb, the whole being flanked by an ꜥnḫ and a nfr.
PARALLELS: Design Classes 3B2, 3B6. Giveon, Scarabs British Museum pp. 112-113 no. 6. Petrie, BP I pl. 10:80. Id., AG IV pl. 7:193. Id., AG V pl. 9:75. Matouk, Corpus II p. 412 no. 2409. Tufnell, Lachish IV pls. 30/31:65 and 32/33:79.
DATE: Hyksos, Dyn. XV (ca. 1650-1550 B.C.E.).
PROVENANCE: Area A, locus 1352 (fill with mixed material), level 10.55, stratum A-8; MB to Iron Age (2000-587 B.C.E.). Field no. 11258/80.
COLLECTION: Tel Aviv University, Institute of Archaeology (M. Kochavi).

48

2:1

2:1

49

44 ITEM: Scarab, D8/0/e10, border slightly abraded; linear engraving; fine grey steatite, glazed white; 16.5 x 11 x 6.1 mm.

DECORATION: A nude female figure, the Syrian "naked goddess", standing en face, with arms at sides, and head in profile; the pubic area is represented as a large leaf. The series of oblique strokes on both sides of the figure may indicate twigs (or a giant leaf), between (resp. in front of) which the goddess appears.

PARALLELS: Design Class 1B, 10D1. Petrie, BP I pl. 10:103. Id., BP II pl. 73:12. Tufnell, Lachish IV pl. 30/31:47. Giveon, Scarabs British Museum pp. 114-115 no. 16. Keel, Tell Keisan p. 273, fig. 84.

DATE: Hyksos, Dyn. XV (ca. 1650-1550 B.C.E.).

PROVENANCE: Area A, locus 1384, stratum A-11; MB II B (1750-1550 B.C.E.). Field no. 11351/80.

COLLECTION: Tel Aviv University, Institute of Archaeology (M. Kochavi).

45 ITEM: Scarab, B2/II/e11, slightly burnt (?); linear engraving, with slight hatching; grey steatite; 13.4 x 9.7 x 5.8 mm.

DECORATION: Horizontally arranged: an ibex couchant between two twigs, an upright one before him, an oblique one above his hind quarters.

PARALLELS: Design Class 9B. Petrie, BP I pl. 10:92. Id., AG V pl. 10:118. Giveon, Scarabs British Museum pp. 84-85 no. 69 and pp. 116-117 no. 21. Hornung/Staehelin, Skarabäen Basel no. D 23.

DATE: Hyksos, Dyn. XV (ca. 1600-1550 B.C.E). The humeral callosity on the back of the scarab indicates a date at the close of this period (cf. Ward, StSc I pp. 80-83).

PROVENANCE: Area C, locus 1663; Hellenistic - Roman period (332 B.C.E. - 2nd century C.E.). Field no. 13286/70.

COLLECTION: Tel Aviv University, Institute of Archaeology (M. Kochavi).

46 ITEM: Scarab, head and clypeus partially lost; sunk relief with partial cross hatching; steatite; 13 x 9 x 4 mm.

DECORATION: Horizontally arranged: the divine name *Imn-R^c* (with two determinative strokes on the right of the solar disk), to the left of which is an upended *nb*.

PARALLELS: Tufnell, Lachish IV pls. 37/38:273 and 39/40:373-374.

DATE: Mid-Dyn. XVIII - early Dyn. XX (ca. 1400-1150 B.C.E.).

PROVENANCE: Area X, locus 2959, level 5.13, stratum X-12; LB II B (1300-1150). Field no. 37004/80.

COLLECTION: Tel Aviv University, Institute of Archaeology (M. Kochavi).

47 ITEM: Scarab, B1/II/d5, border abraded; sunk relief, hatching and cross hatching; steatite (?), glazed white; 19.7 x 13.9 x 7.7 mm.

DECORATION: A human figure with a peculiar headdress and large triangular kilt holding an enormous blossom (papyrus or flower) stands atop a *nb*; to the right a lying crocodile.

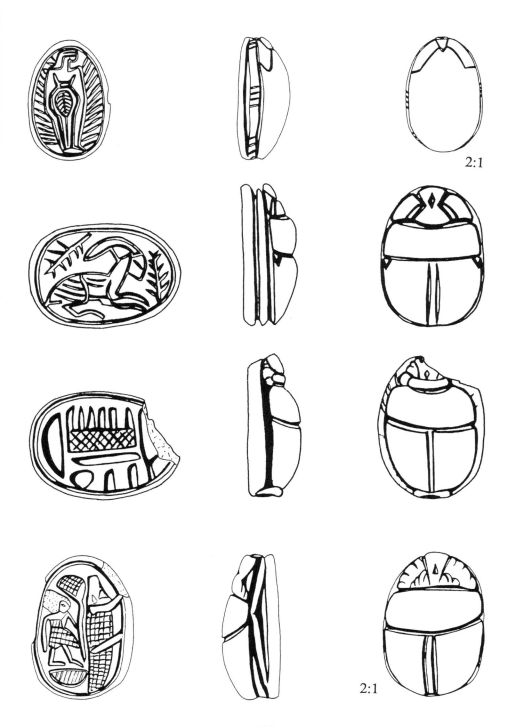

2:1

2:1

51

PARALLELS: Design Class 9D and 10. Petrie, BP II pl. 44:70. Kenyon, Jericho II fig. 303:15.
DATE: Dyn. XII - early Dyn. XIII (ca. 1950-1750 B.C.E.).
PROVENANCE: Area X, locus 1732, stratum X-12; LB II B (1300-1150 B.C.E.). Field no. 37212/50.
COLLECTION: Tel Aviv University, Institute of Archaeology (M. Kochavi).

48   ITEM: Scarab, head and back very rudimentary; linear engraving (deep?); fayence; 14 x 11 x 6 mm.
DECORATION: A kind of Maltese cross with a 'diamond' in the centre.
PARALLELS: Anthes, Mit Rahineh p. 56 and pl. 33:326-328. The Maltese cross seems to have rare antecedants on ancient seals from Crete (cf,. e.g., Matz, CMS I no. 438), Anatolia (cf., e.g., Alp, Karahuyuk pp. 259-261:378.379.389), and Kassite Babylonia (cf., e.g., Vollenweider, Genève no. 58) before becoming a common ornamental design in the Western Mediterranean at the very close of LB II, when frequently used on contemporary pottery (cf., e.g., Amiran, Pottery pls. 90:12 and 93:3).
DATE: End of LB II B - Iron Age II A (ca. 1200-900 B.C.E.).
PROVENANCE: Area X, locus 1732, level 5.75, stratum X-12; LB II B (1300-1150 B.C.E.). Field no. 37248/80.
COLLECTION: Tel Aviv University, Institute of Archaeology (M. Kochavi).

49   ITEM: Cowroid; sunk relief; steatite; 19 x 11 x 6 mm.
DECORATION: The prenomen Nb-$m3^ct$-R^c, i.e. Amenhotep III (1391-1353 B.C.E.); the goddess is holding an $^cn\underline{h}$ on her lap. The royal name is not in a cartouche.
PARALLELS: Hornung/Staehelin, Skarabäen Basel no. 349.
DATE: Second half of Dyn. XVIII (14th cent. B.C.E.).
PROVENANCE: Area X, locus 6024 (pit), stratum X-2; early Arabic Period (690-1099 C.E.). Field no. 43303/70.
COLLECTION: Tel Aviv University, Institute of Archaeology (M. Kochavi).

50   ITEM: Scarab, longitudinally fractured, one half lost; sunk relief; fayence (?), glazed turquoise; 35.7 x 13.5 x 15.2 mm.
DECORATION: The prenomen $[N]b$-$[m3]^ct$-$[R^c]$, i.e. Amenhotep III (1390-1353 B.C.E.); the goddess is holding an $^cn\underline{h}$ on her lap. The royal name is not in a cartouche.
PARALLELS: Tufnell, Lachish IV pl. 37/38:292.
DATE: Second half of Dyn. XVIII (14th cent. B.C.E.).
PROVENANCE: Area X, locus 6038 (wall foundation), stratum X-2; early Arabic Period (690-1099 C.E.). Field no. 43333/70.
COLLECTION: Tel Aviv University, Institute of Archaeology (M. Kochavi).

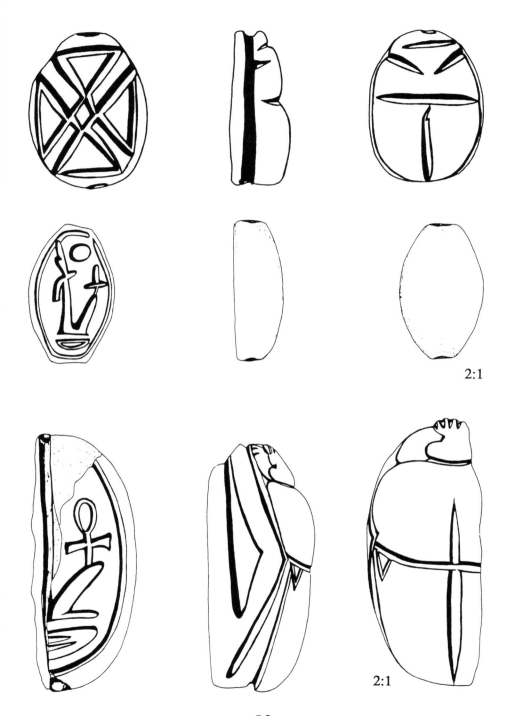

2:1

2:1

53

51   ITEM: Scarab, D6/0/d5, slightly damaged; linear engraving, partially hatched; steatite; 16 x 13 x 8 mm.
DECORATION: Horizontally arranged: a double Z-spiral is framed by two symmetrical plants on *nb*, each having an upright stalk inside and a bent and bound one outside.
PARALLELS: Design Classes 2A, 3A2. Petrie, AG II pl. 8:152. Id., BP I pl. 12:131. Giveon, Scarabs British Museum pp. 142-143 no. 14. Tufnell, Lachish IV pl. 34/35:156.
DATE: Dyn. XI-XV (ca. 2050-1550 B.C.E.)
PROVENANCE: Area X, locus 6008 (mixed material); LB to Iron Age (1550-587 B.C.E.). Field no. 45438/70.
COLLECTION: Tel Aviv University, Institute of Archaeology (M. Kochavi).

52   ITEM: Scarab, ?/0/e10, head and back partially lost due to diagonal fracture; linear engraving, with cross hatching; steatite; *12 x 11 x 8 mm.
DECORATION: A male figure in a knee-length kilt facing an uraeus to the right (both heads are missing).
PARALLELS: Design Class 10. Tufnell, Lachish IV pls. 32/33:72. Vodoz, Genève no. 35.
DATE: Dyn. XII-XIII (ca. 1950-1650 B.C.E.).
PROVENANCE: Area X, locus 4602, stratum X-12; LB II B (1300-1150 B.C.E.). Field no. 45653/70.
COLLECTION: Tel Aviv University, Institute of Archaeology (M. Kochavi).

53   ITEM: Scarab, one side damaged; sunk relief, scratched hatching; grey-brown steatite; 21.7 x 15.8 x *7 mm.
DECORATION: On the left an uraeus, probably *nṯr nfr* "good god" above it; on the right, below an unclear sign, a cartouche with inscription $Wsr-m3^ct-R^c$ $stp-n-R^c$, i.e. the prenomen and epithet of Ramesses II (1279-1213 B.C.E.); beneath these is probably a *nb*.
DATE: Dyn. XIX, Ramesses II (ca. 1279-1213 B.C.E.) or later.
PROVENANCE: Area X, locus 4805 (fill of mixed material), stratum X-5 (?); LB to Iron Age (1550-587 B.C.E.). Field no. 47027/70.
COLLECTION: Tel Aviv University, Institute of Archaeology (M. Kochavi).

54   ITEM: Scarab, border slightly abraded; linear engraving; steatite (?), glazed white, fayence glaze on back; 19.2 x 13.3 x 8.8 mm.
DECORATION: Two groups of intricate interlocking Z-spirals joined by an oblique, elongated spiral.
PARALLELS: Design Class 2B1. Kenyon, Jericho II figs. 294:1, 296:1 and 297:8. Rowe, Catalogue no. 401 (Bet Shean).
DATE: Dyn. XII-XV (ca. 1950-1550 B.C.E.).
PROVENANCE: Area X, locus 4823, stratum X-11; early Iron Age I (12th cent. B.C.E.). Field no. 47182/70.
COLLECTION: Tel Aviv University, Institute of Archaeology (M. Kochavi).

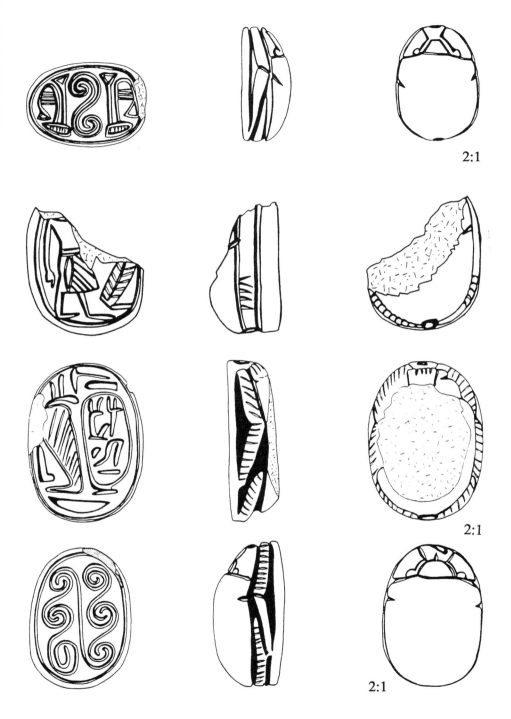

2:1

2:1

2:1

55   ITEM: Scarab, A6/0/e6b; linear engraving; steatite (?), glazed white; 16.5 x 11.2 x 7.5 mm.
DECORATION: At the top *nsw-bity*, "King of Upper and Lower Egypt"; below *ḫpr* and *ḏd*, symmetrically flanked by *wḏ3t*, *k3* and (probably) bent *w3s*-sceptres.
PARALLELS: Design Class 3. Kenyon, Jericho II fig. 288:10.
DATE: Dyn. XII-XV (ca. 1950-1550 B.C.E.).
PROVENANCE: Area X, locus 6046 (mixed material), stratum X-15; MB - LB (2000-1150 B.C.E.). Field no. 47456/70.
COLLECTION: Tel Aviv University, Institute of Archaeology (M. Kochavi).

56   ITEM: Scarab; linear engraving; steatite, glazed white; 18 x 12.6 x 7.4 mm.
DECORATION: A series of hooked curved lines, parallel and perpendicular to one another, provide a frame for two very small, symmetrically set *nfr*.
PARALLELS: Design Class 2B2. Petrie, AG IV pls. 9:293 and 11:437.
DATE: Dyn. XII-XV (ca. 1950-1550 B.C.E.).
PROVENANCE: Area C-2, locus 6718; late Roman period (2nd-3rd cent. C.E.). Field no. 58116/80.
COLLECTION: Tel Aviv University, Institute of Archaeology (M. Kochavi).

Tel Arad

Y. Aharoni and R. Amiran started excavations at Tel Arad (the biblical Arad) in 1962 on behalf of the Israel Exploration Society, the Hebrew University (Jerusalem) and the Israel Department of Antiquities. With the occasional assistance of M. Kochavi, the excavations continued intermittently into the 1970's, showing that the original settlement during the Early Bronze Age found its successor only in the early part of the Iron Age, following which the tell was almost continually in use until modern times. The scarabs which we are able to present here through the generosity of Mrs. M. Aharoni were found in the course of the excavations on top of the mound in Iron Age strata.

57   ITEM: Scarab, severely abraded; linear engraving; steatite; 21.3 x 14.3 x 9.7 mm.
DECORATION: Three vertical columns of hieroglyphs and pseudo-hieroglyphs, predominantly *ᶜnḫ*-signs; above, a legless flying bird on the left, a bird (?) in the middle and a circle on the right; in the middle of the composition a *nsw*, perhaps a *ḫrw*-oar and an *ᶜnḫ*; below a winged *ᶜnḫ* (?) protecting further signs of uncertain character. Without any apparent border line.
DATE: Most probably Dyn. XXV-XXVI (ca. 750-525 B.C.E.).

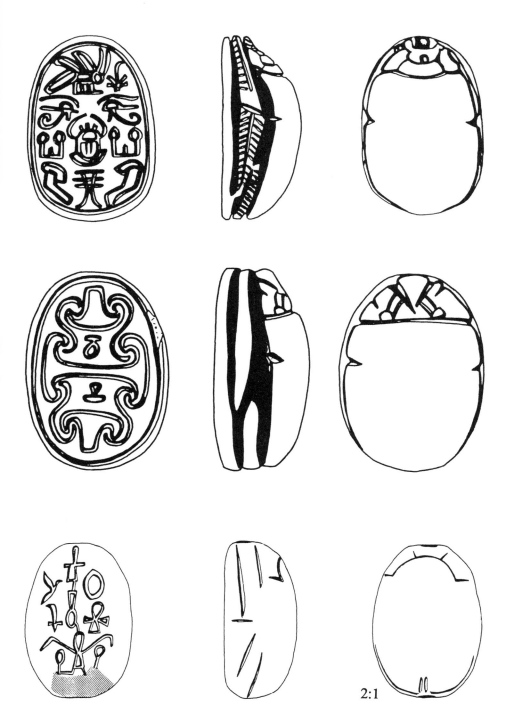

2:1

57

PROVENANCE: Fortress, locus 380, stratum IX; early Iron Age II C (ca. 800-734 B.C.E.). Field no. 1589/51.
COLLECTION: Tel Aviv University, Institute of Archaeology, IDAM 67-219.

58 ITEM: Stamp seal in the form of a crouching lion, fragmentary; schematic sunk relief, almost linear; grey steatite, glazed white; *17.2 x *10.2 x *19.6 mm.
DECORATION: Horizontally arranged; a striding lion heads for a geometric pattern derived of a Red Crown at the right. Above the lion's head and neck are traces of further design elements.
PARALLELS: Giveon, BIES 25 (1961) pp. 249-250. Petrie, AG IV pl. 11:415. Rowe, Catalogue no. S.54 (Beth Shean). Lamon, Megiddo Water System pl. 8: 5. Matouk collection no. M.2641. Hornung/Staehelin, Skarabäen Basel no. 347. Tufnell, Lachish III pl. 34:25. Lamon/Shipton, Megiddo I pls. 69:59 and 71:59. Coldstream, Madrider Beiträge 8 (1982) p. 264 and pl. 25:c. Schuhmacher, Mutesellim I pl. 26:o. A group of similarly shaped seals has apparently been found in a recent excavation in Iran in a context dating to ca. 1000-800 B.C.E. (personal communication M.I. Marcus, Philadelphia, 16.2.85).
DATE: Iron Age I - II A (ca. 1150-900 B.C.E.).
PROVENANCE: Fortress, locus 903, stratum XII; Iron Age I (ca. 1150-1000 B.C.E.) [or late Iron Age I - II A (11th-10th cent. B.C.E.)]. Field no. 6500/50.
COLLECTION: Tel Aviv University, Institute of Archaeology.

59 ITEM: Scarab; sunk relief, moderate depth; steatite; 15.2 x 10.8 x 7.1 mm.
DECORATION: In the upper register a sphinx with an unclear sign above his hind quarters (probably derived from the $ḥs$-vase or the $ḥm$-club, but actually more similar to the $šn$-ring); below a plant (?) or an $^cnḫ$-sign beside a $w3ḏ$-plant; between them an oval or t above three vertical strokes. The reading $ḥsy nb t3.wy$, "he whom the Lord of the Two Lands praises" (reading the two plants beneath the sphinx as those representing Upper and Lower Egypt, while the sphinx itself would represent the value nb), disregards the signs in the middle of the lower register, while retaining the meaning of numerous parallels. Interpreting "the Majesty of the Lord of the Two Lands" faces the same problem.
PARALLELS: Petrie, Hyksos and Israelite Cities pl. 33:39. Id., BP I pl. 43: 530. Newberry, CG pls. 14:36607 and 17:37370. Matouk, Corpus II p. 385: 610. Giveon, Scarabs British Museum pp. 152-153 no. 52. See also Leclant, Kition II pp. 69-70 no. Kit. 800 with further parallels.
DATE: Dyn. XXI-XXIV (ca. 1175-716 B.C.E.).
PROVENANCE: Fortress, locus 514 (wall foundations), stratum IX; early Iron Age II C (ca. 800-734 B.C.E.). Field no. 1270/50.
COLLECTION: Tel Aviv University, Institute of Archaeology, IDAM 67-620.

60 ITEM: Scarab, severely abraded; shallow relief (?); blue paste or fayence; 11.8 x 8.3 x 5.4 mm.
DECORATION: An $^cnḫ$-sign before a bird, below which is a papyrus plant with

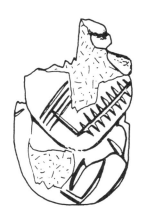

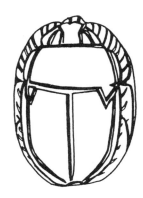

three blossoms (ḫ3), beside an i-reed or, more probably, a sw. Without any apparent border line.
PARALLELS: Vercoutter, Objets égyptiens no. 395.
DATE: Most probably Dyn. XXVI (ca. 664-525 B.C.E.).
PROVENANCE: Fortress, fill, from brick wall foundations, unstratified; Iron Age II C (8th-6th cent. B.C.E.). Field no. 773/50.
COLLECTION: Tel Aviv University, Institute of Archaeology, IDAM 67-621.

61   ITEM: Scaraboid; linear, cross strokes, partially hatched; black limestone (?); 14.3 x 10.6 x 9.1 mm.
DECORATION: A semi-circle design, probably a crescent moon, is set above an object bearing a certain resemblance to a Cretan double axe. The haft however does not extend through the piece as is customary in representations of such, and the cross hatching is not symmetrical, as might be expected. It is suggested that the design should be interpreted as a crescent moon above an altar, the nature of which was perhaps no longer clear to the seal-cutter. No border line.
PARALLELS: Vollenweider, Genève no. 77. Keel, Jahwe-Visionen und Siegel-kunst pp. 288-295 and pls. IVb & Va. Weippert, BN 5 (1978) pp. 56-57. Matz, CMS XII nos. 182 and 193. Keel, Tell Keisan pp. 274-275 and 279-281, figs. 88.90.91 with pls. 89:16 and 24.
DATE: Iron Age I - II B (ca. 1150-800 B.C.E.).
PROVENANCE: Fortress, locus 790, stratum VIII; early Iron Age II C (ca. 734-701 B.C.E.). Field no. 6386/50.
COLLECTION: Tel Aviv University, Institute of Archaeology.

Khorbat ᶜErav

(arabic Khirbet ᶜArvin, 2 km. north/north-east of Kibbutz Elon; 1715/2765)

62   ITEM: Scarab, base damaged; sunk relief, cross strokes; 15 x 11 x 7 mm.
DECORATION: Horizontally arranged: a long-legged bird, probably a goose, moves to the right towards a twig-like plant; above its back is a horizontal line which might be a debased form of the nb-sign or a simple n, in any case to be read as part of the divine name Imn. A further sign to the right of the stalk has been lost. If a goose, the creature could represent Amun.
PARALLELS: Hornung/Staehelin, Skarabäen Basel nos. 434-435. Petrie, BP II pl. 55:274. Id., Memphis I pl. 34:82 and 84. Id., AG II pls. 7:11.71 and 8:111. Vodoz, Genève no. F 18. Loud, Megiddo II pl. 149:1.
DATE: Dyn. XIX - early Dyn. XXI (ca. 1295-1000 B.C.E.).
PROVENANCE: No stratified context; surface find (?).
COLLECTION: Unknown.

 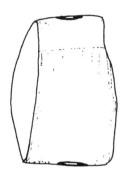 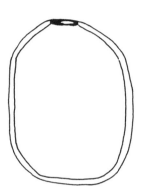

Ḥanita

(1665/2770)

63   ITEM: Scarab, edges battered; partially sunk relief with hatching, partially linear engraving; steatite, glazed white; 15.5 x 11.1 x 8.5 mm.
DECORATION: Within a border of eight separate double-ringed concentric circles and one single circle with point is a seated figure holding an object, perhaps a knife or dagger, being the typical hieroglyphic representation of a "guardian". This can be interpreted as meaning Egyptian *s3w*, which is closely related to the word for amulet and thus well suited for the decoration of a seal amulet.
PARALLELS: For the border of concentric circles see Petrie, BP II pl. 50:45. Tufnell, Lachish IV pls. 30/31:1 and 32/33:134.
DATE: Dyn. XVIII-XIX (1540-1186 B.C.E.). The use of a border consisting of concentric circles of this type would appear to be typical of late Dyn. XVIII and Dyn. XIX, although the principle originated already in Dyn. XI, and was taken up as well by Hyksos scarab-cutters of Dyn. XV.
PROVENANCE: Surface find.
COLLECTION: Kibbutz Ḥanita. IDAM 75-חן (Neg.-no. 50531-32).

64   ITEM: Scarab; sunk relief, partially hatched; steatite; 14.9 x 10.9 x 6.5 mm.
DECORATION: In a horizontally set cartouche, the prenomen $Mn-k3[.w]-R^c$, i.e. Mykerinos, the 5th king of Dyn. IV (2640-2520 B.C.E.). At this early time there were no scarabs made; for an unknown reason the name of this king is however often found on scarabs of Dyn. XXVI (see Hall, Catalogue nos. 32.34. 35.38.41. Vercoutter, Objets égyptiens nos. 372-382). Below the cartouche stands Horus in falcon form upon a pedestal, with a flail on his back. Behind him is Sakhmet (lion-headed in a tight dress) holding a long-stemmed flower in one out-stretched hand, while the other hand is relaxed. The falcon with flail and Sakhmet are both equally typical of Dyn. XXVI (Petrie, Naukratis I pl. 37:58-61 and 131. Vercoutter, Objets égyptiens nos. 89-92. 94.66-69). Below is a *nb*-sign.
DATE: Dyn. XXVI (664-525 B.C.E.).
PROVENANCE: Surface find.
COLLECTION: Kibbutz Ḥanita, IDAM 75-חן (Neg.-no. 50533-34).

Tell Jerishe

Between 1927 and 1940, E.L. Sukenik directed four campaigns of excavations at this double tell on behalf of the Department of Archaeology of the Hebrew University (Jerusalem). His 1951 campaign concentrated on the major MB II glacis fortification sys-

tem of the tell, which emphasized the significance of Tell Jerishe in that period. Evidence was found of a smaller settlement of MB I and MB II A. After the destruction of the MB II town at the beginning of the Late Bronze Age (perhaps in connexion with the Egyptian campaigns in pursuit of the Hyksos leaders in their Palestinian strongholds), a city flourished once again in the later part of this period. The Philistine village which arose upon the ruins of the LB town was in its turn likewise destroyed and a new Israelite city established there. In Iron Age II this settlement was razed and the tell not settled again except briefly in the Abbaside period of the 9th-10th centuries C.E.

The material wealth of these various settlements has been brought to light in the recent excavations conducted at Tell Jerishe by the Archaeological Expedition to the Coastal Plain of Israel, headed by Dr. Z. Herzog of the Institute of Archaeology of Tel Aviv University and Prof. J. Muhly of the University of Pennsylvania, in 1980-1983. While a justly renowned heart scarab of the late New Kingdom with a spell (no. 30 of the Book of the Dead defending its owner against a possibly treacherous heart in the Other World) was found in the earlier excavations, a number of other interesting scarabs have been found in the new excavations. We are able to present them here thanks to the generosity of Dr. Z. Herzog.

65   ITEM: Scarab, D8/0/e5, border abraded and slightly damaged; linear engraving with partial hatching; grey steatite, glazed white; 16.8 x 12.3 x 7.9 mm.
      DECORATION: Above, a *w3ḥ* flanked by two symmetrical uraei turned inwards; separating these from the lower register are two *nb*- or *r*-signs flanking a *t*-shaped sign. Below, a *w3ḏ* between two *ᶜnḥ*-signs, each enclosed in ovals, above an *r* (probably to be understood as an unsuccessful *nb*). The whole may represent little more than an effort to combine a number of lucky signs, as was done so frequently in this period.
      PARALLELS: Design Classes 3B1c, 9C1. Giveon, Scarabs British Museum pp. 64-65 no. 13 and pp. 68-69 no. 27. Petrie, AG III pl. 3:51. Tufnell, Lachish IV pls. 39/40:327.
      DATE: Hyksos, Dyn. XV (ca. 1650-1550 B.C.E.).
      PROVENANCE: Locus 9, surface find. Field no. 34/50.
      COLLECTION: Tel Aviv University, Institute of Archaeology (Z. Herzog).

66   ITEM: Scaraboid (?), ?/0/e2, severely abraded; shallow sunk relief with hatching; black steatite; 13.2 x 9.7 x 4.9 mm.
      DECORATION: Horizontally arranged: a falcon between two symmetrically set uraei turned inwards.
      PARALLELS: Design Class 9C3. Kenyon, Jericho II fig. 301:4. Petrie, AG I pl. 13:60. Id., AG IV pl. 9:319. Buhl/Holm-Nielsen, Shiloh pp. 37-38, fig. 12 and pp. 78-79 with pl. 24:195. Giveon, Scarabs British Museum pp. 120-121 no. 29. Bietak, MDAIK 26 (1970) pl. 19a (above, right).
      DATE: Probably Dyn. XV (ca. 1650-1550 B.C.E.).
      PROVENANCE: Locus 9, surface find. Field no. 34/51.
      COLLECTION: Tel Aviv University, Institute of Archaeology (Z. Herzog).

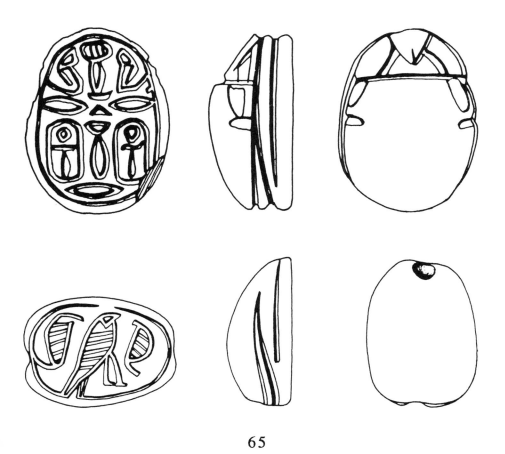

67   ITEM: Scarab, D5/I/e11; linear engraving; reddish brown steatite (?); 11.7 x 7.7 x 6.1 mm.
       DECORATION: A stylized *nwb* sits above a double figure-eight loop, below which is a *nb*.
       PARALLELS: Design Classes 1B, 2, 3. Petrie, AG I pl. 14:156. Id., AG IV pl. 7:144.159.219.267. Tufnell, Lachish IV pls. 36/37:209 and 37/38:320.
       DATE: Hyksos, Dyn. XV (ca. 1650-1540 B.C.E.) or a later imitation of that style.
       PROVENANCE: Locus 9, surface find. Field no. 34/52.
       COLLECTION: Tel Aviv University, Institute of Archaeology (Z. Herzog).

68   ITEM: Scarab, laterally pierced (!), base and border damaged; sunk relief, almost linear; steatite (?), glazed white; 10.4 x 8.5 x 5.2 mm.
       DECORATION: Horizontally arranged, very schematic without border line: a lion passant, with a line (or *nb*) beneath him.
       PARALLELS: See nos. 58 (Arad) and 73 (Jerishe).
       DATE: Iron Age I - II A (1150-900 B.C.E.).
       PROVENANCE: Locus 9, surface find. Field no. 34/53.
       COLLECTION: Tel Aviv University, Institute of Archaeology (Z. Herzog).

69   ITEM: Fragment of a scarab; linear engraving; grey steatite, glazed white; *14 x *8.3 x *6.1 mm.
       DECORATION: A number of rounded, partially interlocking S-spirals.
       PARALLELS: Design Class 2B1. Petrie, AG I pl. 13:66. Id., AG IV pl. 7:233.
       DATE: Dyn. XII-XV (1900-1550 B.C.E.).
       PROVENANCE: Locus 9, surface find. Field no. 34/54.
       COLLECTION: Tel Aviv University, Institute of Archaeology (Z. Herzog).

70   ITEM: Scarab, severely abraded, sides partially lost; partially sunk relief, partially linear engraving; steatite (?), glazed white; 17.6 x 12.2 x 8.3 mm.
       DECORATION: Very schematic, probably the prenomen and epithet $Wsr-m3^ct-R^c stp-n-R^c$, i.e. Ramesses II (1279-1213 B.C.E.), in an oval, with four uraei (?) set above and below. Hooked lines - probably palm-branches, symbols of rejuvenation - fill the remaining space.
       PARALLELS: Jaeger, Scarabées Menkhéperrê figs. 110b & 240. Same design without the oval and name in the centre: Starkey/Harding, BP II pls. 48:23, 50:104 and 55:314 (= Rowe, Catalogue no. 796).
       DATE: LB II B - Iron Age I (ca. 1270-1000 B.C.E.).
       PROVENANCE: Locus 9, surface find. Field no. 34/80.
       COLLECTION: Tel Aviv University, Institute of Archaeology (Z. Herzog).

71   ITEM: Scarab, D4/0/e10, base and border slightly damaged, perhaps prior to glazing; deep linear engraving, hatching; steatite (?), glazed white; 13.8 x 10.4 x 6.8 mm.

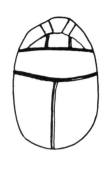

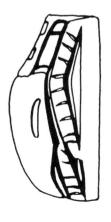
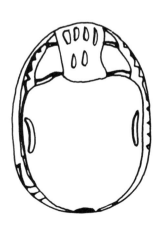

DECORATION: Within a rope border, three signs: perhaps a $ḫ3$, above an $ᶜ$, and an r or nb.
PARALLELS: Design Classes 3, 8A.
DATE: Hyksos, Dyn. XV (ca. 1650-1550 B.C.E.).
PROVENANCE: Area A, locus 73; late MB II B (1650-1550 B.C.E.). Field no. 200/80.
COLLECTION: Tel Aviv University, Institute of Archaeology (Z. Herzog).

72   ITEM: Scarab, D9/II/e11; linear engraving, partially hatched; steatite (?), glazed white; 17.3 x 12.4 x 7.7 mm.
DECORATION: A convoluted coiled pattern with a knot-like central X-cross, and two cross bars, above and below.
PARALLELS: Design Class 6B2a. Giveon, Scarabs British Museum pp. 92-93 nos. 91-94.
DATE: Hyksos, Dyn. XV (ca. 1650-1550 B.C.E.).
PROVENANCE: Area A, Locus 50, surface find. Field no. 518/80.
COLLECTION: Tel Aviv University, Institute of Archaeology (Z. Herzog), IDAM 77-263.

73   ITEM: Scarab; sunk relief; steatite (?), glazed white; 14.4 x 10.8 x 7 mm.
DECORATION: Horizontally arranged: a lion passant with tail above his back, before him a peculiar sign, perhaps a debased i-reed or $m3ᶜt$-feather (or even an uraeus); below are two long thin signs, the lower of which with knobby append-ages possibly to be regarded as an n, the whole thus going back to a Amun-trigram. No border line.
PARALLELS: Petrie, AG II pl. 7:101. Id., AG IV pl. 11:404 and 447. Id., SCN pl. 40:19.3.29. Rowe, Catalogue no. 814 (Beth Shemesh). Tufnell, La-chish III pl. 45:130. Ead., Lachish IV pl. 36/37:216. Giveon, Scarabs British Museum pp. 156-157 no. 5. Hayes, JNES 10 (1951) pl. 176:S 99. A glance at the parallels suggested here indicates that this piece represents a composition ma-de at a time when the original intent of the decoration elements had been long forgotten, but when various symbols could still serve as models.
DATE: Iron Age II A (1000-900 B.C.E.).
PROVENANCE: Area B, locus 160; Iron Age II A (1000-900 B.C.E.). Field no. 1073/80.
COLLECTION: Tel Aviv University, Institute of Archaeology (Z. Herzog).

74   ITEM: Oval plaque, abraded; shallow sunk relief; blue fayence; 13 x 9.75 x 4.3 mm.
DECORATION: Side A: Bereft of border and cartouche is the prenomen Mn-$ḫpr$-$Rᶜ$, i.e. Tuthmosis III (1479-1425 B.C.E.), with the typical royal epithet $nṯr$-nfr, "(the) perfect (or good) god" flanking the beetle. It should be noted that $nṯr$-nfr is primarily a royal and not a divine epithet, so that there is little basis for reading this as a cryptographic writing for Amun. The name is not enclosed within a car-touche (cf. Jaeger, Scarabées Menkhéperrê pp. 159-160 for near contemporary

68

2:1

69

scarabs of Tuthmosis III without the cartouche) nor is there any border line visible. Tuthmosis III was considered by many as a strong martial ruler, aside from being a titulary god, and thus his name was ideal for use on protective amulets. That he was in fact admired and not forgotten outside of Egypt is perhaps best illustrated by the fact that he is the only non-contemporaneous Pharaoh mentioned in the Amarna letters (Knudtzon, EA 59:8 and 55:4). Side B: A four leaved rosette with converging crossed spirals.
PARALLELS: Jaeger, Scarabées Menkhéperrê pp. 169-172 and figs. 7.109-110. 136.237-238. Tufnell, Lachish IV pl. 37/38:299 (= pl. 54:19). Hornung/ Staehelin, Skarabäen Basel no. 338.
DATE: Mid - end of Dyn. XVIII (ca. 1479-1295 B.C.E.).
PROVENANCE: Area C, locus 251; LB (1550-1150 B.C.E.). Field no. 2004/ 80.
COLLECTION: Tel Aviv University, Institute of Archaeology (Z. Herzog).

75   ITEM: Scarab, border slightly abraded; sunk relief, partially hatched; dark steatite, glazed white; 16 x 11.6 x 7.2 mm.
DECORATION: Horizontally arranged: the divine name *Imn-R^c* with several inscrutable signs to the left.
PARALLELS: Tufnell, Lachish IV pl. 37/38:268-270.
DATE: Dyn. XVIII-XIX (ca. 1450-1190 B.C.E.).
PROVENANCE: Area C, locus 311; LB (1550-1150 B.C.E.). Field no. 2545/ 80.
COLLECTION: Tel Aviv University, Institute of Archaeology (Z. Herzog).

76   ITEM: Scarab, border slightly abraded; shallow sunk relief; amethyst; 23.3 x 17.6 x 12.1 mm.
DECORATION: Horizontally arranged: a griffin on its hind legs with outstretched wings rears above an ibex couchant. On the right of the animals is a peculiar sign reminiscent of the *ms*-hieroglyph, with three strands falling from it.
PARALLELS: Loud, Megiddo Ivories pl. 5:4-5. Petrie, AG III pl. 4:127. Parallels are certainly not to be sought in ordinary Egyptian glyptic material, but an unpublished cylinder seal in the collection of Mr. Justus Meyer (Nahariya) would appear to resemble closely the decoration of this scarab. If the date is correct, the inspiration and work is clearly that of the cosmopolitan Levantine coast familiar with Crete and Mesopotamia.
DATE: LB II B (1300-1150 B.C.E.).
PROVENANCE: Area C, locus 310; LB (1550-1150 B.C.E.). Field no. 2547/ 80.
COLLECTION: Tel Aviv University, Institute of Archaeology (Z. Herzog).

77   ITEM: Scarab, human headed/H/d6, border slightly abraded; sunk relief, partially hatched, cross strokes; grey steatite; 19.4 x 13.6 x 8 mm.
DECORATION: A kneeling male human figure in a short kilt and with a very schematic head (maybe a falcon's head) has placed his left hand upon the neck of

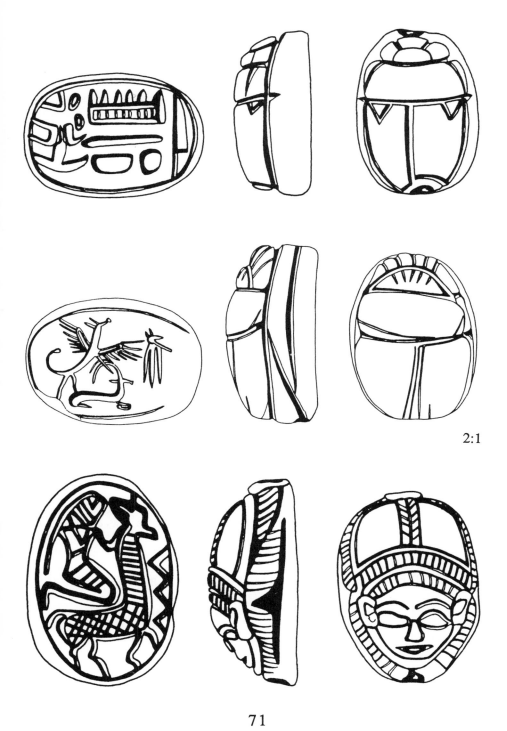

2:1

71

a creature with the body of a horse and the neck and head of a giraffe. In front of this creature is a vertical zigzag line, resembling the hieroglyphic *n*, which is however seldom written upended on scarabs. The scene does not represent a rider on horseback as riding was unknown in Egypt and Palestine in the first half of the second millennium B.C.E. It is probable that our piece is more closely related to those with humans, often falcon-headed, and crocodiles (see above no. 42 [Aphek]) than to those with narrative scenes.

PARALLELS: Back: Petrie, AG III pl. 3:2. Id., AG IV pl. 5:96. Id., SCN pl. 68:R 42. Hornung/Staehelin, Skarabäen Basel no. 912. Staehelin, Pillendreher pp. 20-21. Hayes, Scepter of Egypt II p. 345, fig. 217 (upper right).

DATE: Dyn. XIII-XV (ca. 1750-1550 B.C.E.).

PROVENANCE: Area C, locus 309; LB (1550-1150 B.C.E.). Field no. 2551/50.

COLLECTION: Tel Aviv University, Institute of Archaeology (Z. Herzog).

78   ITEM: Scarab with remains of a bronze ring; shallow sunk relief, hatching; steatite (?), glazed white; 13.4 x 10.7 x 6 mm.

DECORATION: Horizontally arranged: a falcon-headed but wingless griffon wearing a vestigial Red Crown, with extended forepaws; before him perhaps a *k3* but more probably a debased uraeus, beneath him a *nfr*, above his back a *ntr*, behind which is another uraeus. The most probable intent of the decoration was to unite a number of signs representing mundane and divine power.

PARALLELS: Cf. Design Class 9F. Petrie, AG I pl. 14:84 and 165. Id., AG II pl. 7:102. Id., AG III pl. 4:123. Id., AG IV pls. 5:6 and 11:466. Giveon, Scarabs British Museum pp. 82-83 no. 65.

DATE: Ramesside (ca. 1295-1070 B.C.E.) or slightly earlier.

PROVENANCE: Area C, locus 316; LB (1550-1150 B.C.E.). Field no. 2572/80.

COLLECTION: Tel Aviv University, Institute of Archaeology (Z. Herzog).

79   ITEM: Scarab, B8/0/e10; linear engraving, hatching and cross hatching; fayence; 29 x 21 x 12 mm.

DECORATION: Within a border of interlocking Z-spirals is an oval, within this a human figure striding to the left whose head is in profile, with one arm holding a branch. Beneath the feet of the figure a *nb*.

PARALLELS: Design Classes 7A2a, 10A1f. Tufnell, Lachish IV pl. 30/31:45.

DATE: Dyn. XII-XV (ca. 1900-1550 B.C.E.).

PROVENANCE: Area C, locus 700; LB (1550-1150 B.C.E.). Field no. 4521/80.

COLLECTION: Tel Aviv University, Institute of Archaeology (Z. Herzog).

80   ITEM: Amulet in the form of an *wd3t*-eye; fayence; 18 x 13 x   mm.

DECORATION: An uraeus above a lotus blossom. No border line.

DATE: LB II (1400-1150 B.C.E.).

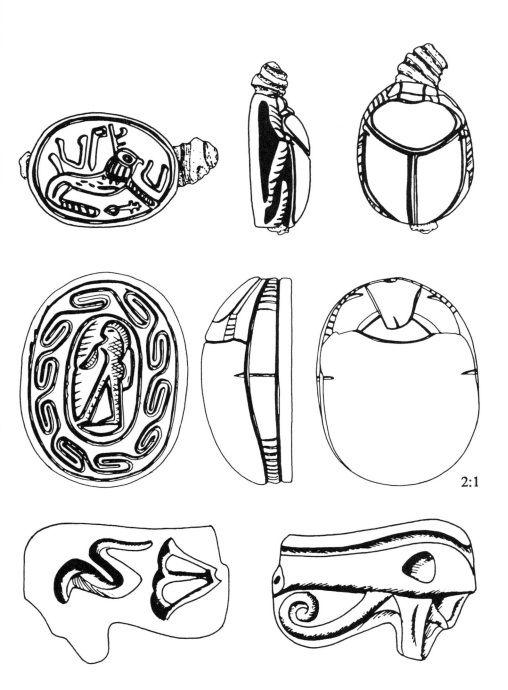

PROVENANCE: Area C, locus 735; LB (1550-1150 B.C.E.). Field no. 4696/
80.
COLLECTION: Tel Aviv University, Institute of Archaeology (Z. Herzog).

81   ITEM: Scarab, D8/0/o; linear engraving, partially hatched; steatite, glazed white;
      13 x 10 x 7 mm.
      DECORATION: Beneath a *ḥtp*, and above a malformed *nb* or *r*, three hiero-
      glyphs: a *ḥm*, an *m* and a *nṯr*. A number of readings are possible, none parti-
      cularly plausible: *ḥm* can mean "majesty" or "servant"; *nṯr*, "god" or "divine";
      and *ḥtp*, "offering" or "peace". While *ḥm-nṯr* meaning "prophet" or "priest" is ra-
      rely written this way, *ḥtp-nṯr* meaning "divine offerings" would be strangely di-
      vided. Each individual sign could represent the protective power of the thing for
      which it stands; this would however leave the *m* strangely inexplicable, but not
      without parallels. Combining the signs to the reading *imy-r ḥm-nṯr ḥtp-<nṯr>*,
      "Steward of the Prophet(?) of <Divine(?)> Offerings", might offer an alternative.
      PARALLELS: Design Class 3. Kenyon, Jericho II fig. 286:7. Petrie, AG III pl.
      4:120.
      DATE: Hyksos, Dyn. XV (ca. 1650-1550 B.C.E.).
      PROVENANCE: Area D, locus 806; Iron Age I (1150-1000 B.C.E.). Field no.
      5454/80.
      COLLECTION: Tel Aviv University, Institute of Archaeology (Z. Herzog).

82   ITEM: Scarab with gold setting, D8/II/-, border partly abraded; linear engraving;
      fayence; 12 x 7 x 5 mm.
      DECORATION: Horizontally arranged: a *w3ḏ* between two *ꜥnḫ*-signs.
      PARALLELS: Design Class 3A3. Petrie, AG II pl. 7:9. Id., AG III pl. 4:142.
      Id., AG IV pl. 5:107.
      DATE: Dyn. XV (ca. 1650-1550 B.C.E.) or rather later.
      PROVENANCE: Area C, locus 1202; LB II (1400-1150 B.C.E.). Field no.
      7052/80.
      COLLECTION: Tel Aviv University, Institute of Archaeology (Z. Herzog).

83   ITEM: Scarab, D8/0/e11; linear engraving; steatite; 16 x 10 x 7 mm.
      DECORATION: A woven cord pattern with central twist.
      PARALLELS: Design Class 6C2. Giveon, Scarabs British Museum pp. 94-95
      no. 100.
      DATE: Hyksos, Dyn. XV (ca. 1650-1550 B.C.E.).
      PROVENANCE: Area D, locus 1303; Iron Age I (1150-1000 B.C.E.). Field no.
      7546/50.
      COLLECTION: Tel Aviv University, Institute of Archaeology (Z. Herzog).

84   ITEM: Scarab, D9(?)/0/e4, base and border damaged; linear engraving, cross stro-
      kes; steatite; 14 x 9 x 6 mm.
      DECORATION: A symmetrically arranged anra group (*nb, n, ꜥ, n, nb/r*).
      PARALLELS: Design Class 3C. Tufnell, Lachish IV pl. 30/31:21.

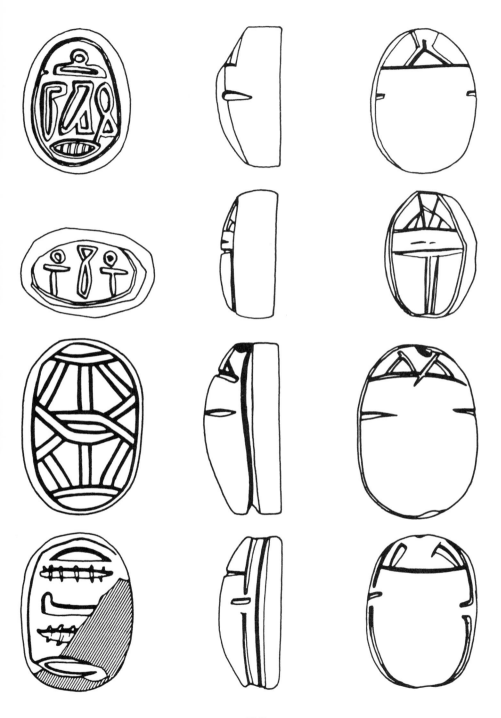

DATE: Hyksos, Dyn. XV (ca. 1650-1550 B.C.E.).
PROVENANCE: Area D, locus 1334; unstratified. Field no. 7647/80.
COLLECTION: Tel Aviv University, Institute of Archaeology (Z. Herzog).

85   ITEM: Ring; sunk relief; Ø 17.6 mm., besel 13.6 x 7 mm.
DECORATION: Three hieroglyphic signs; one reading, however improbable, could be $š3$-mry-$š3$ or $š3$-n-$š3$ for Sheshonk (biblical Shishak), a name borne by a number of Pharaohs of Dyn. XXII-XXIII (945-730 B.C.E.). Equally improbable would be $ḫ3st$-n-$ḫ3st$, for "country of countries" or a nisbe rendering of this, i.e. "(the man of the) country of countries". No border line.
PARALLELS: Hall, Catalogue nos. 2398.2400-2406. Matouk, Corpus I p. 197:754 and 756-758.
DATE: ?
PROVENANCE: Area B, locus 1135; Iron Age I (1150-1000 B.C.E.). Field no. 7809.
COLLECTION: Tel Aviv University, Institute of Archaeology (Z. Herzog).

86   ITEM: Amulet in the form of an $wḏ3t$-eye; back without decoration; bronze; 12.6 x 8 mm.
PARALLELS: Tufnell, Lachish IV pl. 29:56-57.67-68. Gamer-Wallert, Iberische Halbinsel pl. 46.
DATE: LB II - Iron Age II B (1400-800 B.C.E.).
PROVENANCE: Locus 9, surface find. Field no. 2/60.
COLLECTION: Tel Aviv University, Institute of Archaeology (Z. Herzog).

87   ITEM: Plastic human figure with back column, bent legs and hands crossed before the abdomen; neck pierced for suspension; fayence; 42 x 16.6 mm.
This represents a so-called Ptah-Sokar-Osiris statuette, named παταικος after the reference in Herodotus (III:37) referring to the statue of Ptah in Memphis. Ptah was the patron-god of the craftsmen in ancient Egypt and dwarfs were particularly employed for the manufacture of jewelry, so that the resemblance to the Greek Hephaistos may not be coincidental. This does not however explain the amuletic character of these figures, which were distributed not just along the Levantine Coast (cf., e.g., Tufnell, Lachish IV pl. 29), but throughout the Mediterranean basin by the Phoenicians (cf., e.g., Popham/Sackett, Lefkandi I pls. 186:32.17 and 235a (left). Gamer-Wallert, Iberische Halbinsel pls. 36-37). Their identification with a form of Horus-the-child or the protective Bes would actually be more suitable.
DATE: LB II - Iron Age II B (1400-800 B.C.E.).
PROVENANCE: Area A, locus 104, surface find. Field no. 536/80.
COLLECTION: Tel Aviv University, Institute of Archaeology (Z. Herzog).

88   ITEM: Flat amulet; fayence; 13.3 x 6 mm.
Plaque in the form of a malformed bearded male human figure with an unclear headdress, flat arms bent, thus probably representing the god Bes.

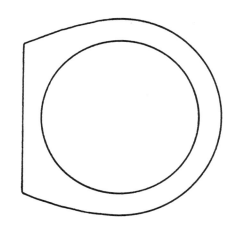

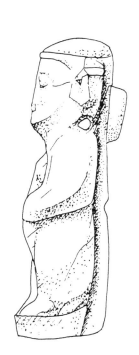

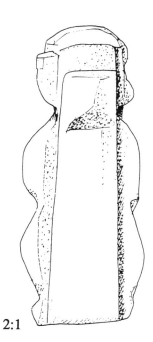

2:1

77

DATE: LB II (1400-1150 B.C.E.).
PROVENANCE: Area C, locus 259; LB II (1400-1150 B.C.E.). Field no. 2073/80.
COLLECTION: Tel Aviv University, Institute of Archaeology (Z. Herzog).

89   ITEM: Fragment of plastic figure, head and shoulders preserved; head laterally pierced for suspension; fayence; 16.6 x 9.3 mm.
DATE: LB II - Iron Age II B (ca. 1400-800 B.C.E.).
PROVENANCE: Area B, locus 1050; Iron Age II A (1000-900 B.C.E.). Field no. 6260/80.
COLLECTION: Tel Aviv University, Institute of Archaeology (Z. Herzog).

90   ITEM: Statuette; fayence; 19 x 8 mm.
Plastic figure of a youth with bent legs and hands crossed before the abdomen. Fitted behind the neck with an eye for suspension.
See above no. 87 for discussion!
DATE: LB II B - Iron Age II (ca. 1300-800 B.C.E.).
PROVENANCE: Area B, locus 547; Iron Age I (1150-1000 B.C.E.). Field no. 6467/80.
COLLECTION: Tel Aviv University, Institute of Archaeology (Z. Herzog).

Tel Kabri

(5 km. north-east of Nahariya; 1643/2695)

Dr. M.W. Prausnitz carried out two excavations at Tel Kabri in 1958 on behalf of the Israel Department of Antiquities and in 1975 with the cooperation of Dr. Aaron Kempinski of the Institute of Archaeology of Tel Aviv University. The following scarab was found at the surface of the tell by Sh. Bar from Moshav Ben-Ammi.

91   ITEM: Scarab, B5/0/d5, slightly abraded; linear engraving; frit; 15 x 10 x 7 mm.
DECORATION: Horizontally arranged, within an interlocking Z-spiral border is the *nwb*-sign and the solar disk. The arrangement and choice of signs seems rather unusual.
PARALLELS: Design Classes 2B2, 3B6. Solar disk associated with a single additional sign within a spiral or scroll border: Petrie, AG II pl. 8:144. Tufnell, Lachish IV pl. 34:145. Bietak, MDAIK 23 (1968) pl. 32c (right) and d (lower left). See below no. 105 (Lachish).
DATE: Dyn. XIII-XV (ca. 1750-1550 B.C.E.).
PROVENANCE: East side of the tell, surface find.
COLLECTION: Unknown.

79

Khirbet Karkara

(1 km. north-north-west of Kibbutz Elon; 1707/2755)

92   ITEM: Scarab, back slightly damaged, edges battered; sunk relief, hatching; 14.5 x 9.7 x 7 mm.
DECORATION: The divine name *Imn-R^c*. A lotus bud with a bent stem flanks the name on the left, a *nb* appears below. The lotus could actually be understood as referring to Amun-Re^c as the saviour (*nḥm*, with the lotus bud as determinative, see Wb. II 296,10).
PARALLELS: Hornung/Staehelin, Skarabäen Basel nos. 607-610 and MV 9. Tufnell, Lachish IV pl. 37/38:271. Starkey/Harding, BP II pls. 49 bottom right, 53:184 and 57:351. Petrie, Memphis I pl. 34:31.38. Id., AG II pl. 7:28.40. Matthiae Scandone, Cagliari no. B 1. The diverse forms indicate that the Egyptians were consciously engaged in word-plays, being especially fond of substituting the *i* -reed with the *m3^{c}t*-feather.
DATE: Dyn. XVIII (ca. 1540-1295 B.C.E.).
PROVENANCE: Byzantine tomb or cave.
COLLECTION: Kibbutz Elon.

Tel Lachish

After the Wellcome-Marston Excavations in the 1930's, directed by J. L. Starkey, the identity of Tell ed-Duweir with biblical Lachish was firmly established. The intrinsic interest of the site encouraged Prof. D. Ussishkin of Tel Aviv University to resume excavations here in the 1970's. These excavations have been very successful, bringing to light further Middle Bronze Age structures including a major palace. Among the finds have been a number of scarabs, and we are obliged to Prof. Ussishkin for permitting us to publish them here. Among those already published is the first piece, a seal impression from a jar in level VII, for which a date somewhat earlier than that already suggested might be advocated. This is not without interest, as this piece could play a certain role in the dating and history of the transitional MB/LB levels at Lachish.

93   ITEM: Impression of an oval seal with linear engraving and hatching; clay; 16 x 11 mm.

DECORATION: A solar barque with disk resting upon the water-sign, above a column of indistinct signs (R^c, t, p, t?), flanked by two uraei rising from above a division bar, below which, probably a $ḥb$-festival-sign (or a simple nb?). Before the uraei may have been two $m3^ct$-feathers, the left one being clearer than the postulated right one.

The solar barque might be unexpected in this chronological context, but it is clearly shown on a parallel (Hayes, Scepter of Egypt I 343, fig. 226 [at top, fourth from left]) revealing in conjunction with the parallels from Jericho Group II tombs that the clearer forms should be dated earlier, and that the solar barque slowly disappears from the repertoire during the Second Intermediate period, only to reappear much later.

PARALLELS: Design Class 3A3. Hall, Catalogue no. 34. Giveon, Scarabs British Museum pp. 176-177 no. 1. For the shape and date of the solar barque cf. esp. Kenyon, Jericho II figs. 284:3, 285:7, 292:9.15, 293:4.8, 295:6.

DATE: Dyn. XIII - early Dyn. XV (ca. 1750-1600 B.C.E.).

PROVENANCE: Area P, locus 3143, level P-4 (= VIII); MB II B (1750-1550 B.C.E.). Field no. 9732/1.

COLLECTION: Tel Aviv University, Institute of Archaeology (D. Ussishkin).

BIBLIOGRAPHY: Ussishkin, Tel Aviv 5 (1978) pp. 9-10, pl. 3:3. Giveon, BSFE 81 (1978) p. 10 with fig. 8.

94   ITEM: Scarab, back severely damaged; sunk relief; steatite, glazed white, traces of hematite; 18.3 x 14.4 x 8.2 mm.

DECORATION: Horizontally arranged: the Pharaoh, wearing a blue crown with uraeus, stands with drawn bow shooting a lion which sits on his hind legs; above and below are five branches. Above this scene are two hieroglyphic signs probably to be read R^c nfr, "the good (sun-god) Re^c". Behind the king is a strange cross-like device.

The whole is partly a reference to the Pharaoh's role as the defender of civilization, as wild beasts were regarded as enemies, and partly a demonstration of the Pharaoh's physical prowess, both being ideologically important themes imparting a certain degree of protection to the owner.

PARALLELS: Matouk, Corpus II pp. 169:XE.V6; 369:1652; 403:1695. Keel, ZDPV 93 (1977) pp. 142-143 fig. 8 with pl. 10D. Hornung/Staehelin, Skarabäen Basel no. 662. Jaeger, Scarabées Menkhéperrê fig. 106.

DATE: Ramesside, Dyn. XIX-XX (ca. 1295-1070 B.C.E.).

PROVENANCE: Area S, locus 3617, level VI; late LB II B (ca. 1200-1150 B.C.E.). Field no. 40006/80.

COLLECTION: Tel Aviv University, Institute of Archaeology (D. Ussishkin).

BIBLIOGRAPHY: Ussishkin, Tel Aviv 5 (1978) p. 45 and pl. 16:2. Giveon, BSFE 81 (1978) 12 with fig. 11.

95 ITEM: Scarab, base slightly damaged; steatite (?); measurements?
DECORATION: Above, two uraei turned inwards flanking a sun disk (R^c); in the middle, two $wd3t$-eyes, surmounted by double feathers reminiscent of the Atef crown; below, a vertical column of hieroglyphic signs (h^c, $3ht$, n, ^{c}) between Red Crowns.
PARALLELS: Design Classes 3B3b, 3B4.
DATE: Hyksos, Dyn. XIII-XV (ca. 1750-1550 B.C.E.).
PROVENANCE: ?
COLLECTION: Tel Aviv University, Institute of Archaeology (D. Ussishkin).
BIBLIOGRAPHY: Giveon, BSFE 81 (1978) pp. 7.9-10 with fig. 7.

96 ITEM: Scarab, battered; linear engraving, partially hatched; black steatite, traces of white glaze; 18.2 x 12.6 x 7.2 mm.
DECORATION: Above, a geometric design of a triangle and diagonal strokes being the vestigial remains of a horizontal Red Crown; below, an uraeus whose tail merges into the brow of an $wd3t$-eye behind it. Two water-lines and another sign (a misunderstood nb?) serve as space-fillers. The arrangement of the signs themselves is awkward, but original. The use of the $wd3t$-eye and the uraeus emphasizes the protective role of the scarab.
PARALLELS: Tufnell, Lachish IV pls. 30/31:66 and 39/40:341.350. Petrie, BP I pls. 33:331 and 43:523.
DATE: Dyn. XIX - early Dyn. XXI (ca. 1300-1000 B.C.E.).
PROVENANCE: Area P, locus 3156, level P-4 (= VIII); MB II B (1750-1550 B.C.E.). Field no. 9072/80. The parallels (showing the course of the corruption) as well as the back and sides would support a date later than that demanded by the archaeological context, indicating probably a disturbance.
COLLECTION: Tel Aviv University, Institute of Archaeology (D. Ussishkin).

97 ITEM: Scarab; sunk relief, crude; steatite, glazed white; 15.4 x 11.6 x 7 mm.
DECORATION: On the right a seated figure, holding an ^cnh and wearing a peculiar headdress reminiscent of the ears of Anubis or the Seth creature, but without any indication of the head form peculiar to these. It is possible that the headdress is just a crudely drawn Red Crown. On the left an oval within which is a seated figure, whose head is adorned with two ovals (similar to less successful versions of the full moon lying in a crescent [see the following item no. 98]), seated upon a third oval above a line. Below a common base line is a r or nb.
DATE: Dyn. XVIII-XIX (ca. 1500-1200 B.C.E.).
PROVENANCE: Area P, locus 3162, level VI; late LB II B (ca. 1200-1150 B.C.E.). Field no. 9749/80.
COLLECTION: Tel Aviv University, Institute of Archaeology (D. Ussishkin)

98 ITEM: Scarab, back mostly lost; sunk relief, partially hatched; brown steatite, glazed white; 19.5 x 14.6 x *7 mm.
DECORATION: A divine triad: a god with double-feather crown (Amun?) between two other gods. The one on the left is clearly falcon-headed, the other one

either very awkward or simply unidentifiable. Above the heads of the two subsidiary divinities are pairs of ovals. The possibility that the falcon-headed figure on the left is the Theban Moon-God, Khonsu, with the ovals as a degenerated form of the moon-symbol, has been considered by E. Hornung (Hornung/ Staehelin, Skarabäen Basel p. 320). The figure on the left bears none of the characteristics of a goddess; Mut, the third member of the Theban Triad, with a vulture-head, is thus probably to be discounted.

PARALLELS: There are many cases representing a central god laterally flanked by two gods with solar or lunar disks above their heads, showing various animal forms. See, e.g., Hornung/Staehelin, Skarabäen Basel nos. 655-656. Tufnell, Lachish IV pls. 36/37:240 and 39/40:339.371. Petrie, BDS pl. 15:1044. Rowe, Catalogue nos. 572 and 711. Giveon, Scarabs British Museum pp. 30-31 no. 25 and 180-181 no. 10.

DATE: Dyn. XVIII-XIX (ca. 1400-1200 B.C.E.).

PROVENANCE: Area P, locus 3294, below level VI (i.e., level P-1/2?); LB II (ca. 14th cent. B.C.E.). Field no. 20467/80.

COLLECTION: Tel Aviv University, Institute of Archaeology (D. Ussishkin).

99   ITEM: Scarab; linear engraving, partial hatching and cross hatching; steatite, glazed white; 12.8 x 8.9 x 6.6 mm.

DECORATION: Horizontally arranged: on the left the prenomen *Mn-ḫpr-R^c*, i.e. Tuthmosis III (1479-1425 B.C.E.), in a cartouche, on the right a falcon; between these *ḫprw ḫ^{c}w*, "appearance of the manifestations (or diadems)", the whole group possibly to be read "Tuthmosis III appears as the Manifestation of Horus". A number of parallels hint at the conventional "lord of manifestations (or diadems)" having provided inspiration here.

PARALLELS: Jaeger, Scarabées Menkhéperrê pp. 137 and 156 with ills. 440-444, figs. 202. 206. 212. 214-215. 319. Petrie, SCN pl. 30:18.7.7.

DATE: Mid-Dyn. XVIII (ca. 1479-1400 B.C.E.).

PROVENANCE: Area G, locus 4584, level VI; late LB II B (ca. 1200-1150 B.C.E.). Field no. 31543/80.

COLLECTION: Tel Aviv University, Institute of Archaeology (D. Ussishkin).

100   ITEM: Impression, faint, on stopper, of a seal with linear engraving, partially hatched; unfired clay; ca. 14 x 10 mm.

DECORATION: Horizontally arranged: two bound (?) and bent plants flank three unclear signs above a set of zigzag lines.

PARALLELS: Design Class 1E2. Kenyon, Jericho II fig. 299:6.

DATE: Hyksos, Dyn. XV (ca. 1650-1550 B.C.E.).

PROVENANCE: Area G, locus 4421 (fill), level IV; Iron Age II B (ca. 900-750 B.C.E.). Field no. 38579/1.

COLLECTION: Tel Aviv University, Institute of Archaeology (D. Ussishkin).

101 ITEM: Impression on a jar-handle, of a seal with linear engraving; clay; ca. 18.5 x 11.5 mm.
DECORATION: A geometric pattern with three horizontal registers. For the most part loops and spirals; the lowest register appears to consist of two kneeling human figures, symmetrically facing one another, with stylized Red Crowns behind them. The figures are in the classic position assumed by bound prisoners.
PARALLELS: Tufnell, Lachish IV pl. 30/31:19.
DATE: Dyn. XII-XV (ca. 1900-1550 B.C.E.).
PROVENANCE: Area S, locus 3642, level IV; Iron Age II B (ca. 900-750 B.C.E.). Field no. 40569/1.
COLLECTION: Tel Aviv University, Institute of Archaeology (D. Ussishkin).

102 ITEM: Scarab; sunk relief, crude; steatite, traces of white glaze; 18.3 x 13.8 x 7.7 mm.
DECORATION: Horizontally arranged: on the right the Pharaoh wearing the blue crown with uraeus, his hands raised in gesture of adoration; on the left a winged sphinx wearing an elaborate Atef crown; between the two is an object, perhaps an offering (?). The usual representations show the sphinx protected by a winged uraeus, hovering above it, and it is possible that this theme lay behind the present scene.
PARALLELS: A very similar sphinx is to be found in Matouk, Corpus II p. 385:620. See further Tufnell, Lachish IV pl. 39/40:343. Hornung/Staehelin, Skarabäen Basel nos. 322-323 and A 2. Giveon, Scarabs British Museum pp. 42-45 nos. 61-63.
DATE: Late Dyn. XVIII - Dyn. XX (ca. 1400-1150 B.C.E.).
PROVENANCE: Area S, locus 3612, level VI; late LB II B (ca. 1200-1150 B.C.E.). Field no. 40875/80.
COLLECTION: Tel Aviv University, Institute of Archaeology (D. Ussishkin).

103 ITEM: Scarab, broken lengthwise, only one half remaining; partially linear engraving, partially sunk relief; grey steatite, glazed white; 14 x *5.3 x 5.6 mm.
DECORATION: Almost undistinguishable; in the upper part of the base decoration, one might possibly recognize the remaining left half of an open lotus flower.
PARALLELS:
DATE: Dyn. XIX-XXII (ca. 1292-716 B.C.E.).
PROVENANCE: Area S, locus 3660 (fill), level IV; Iron Age II B (ca. 900-750 B.C.E.). Field no. 41502/80.
COLLECTION: Tel Aviv University, Institute of Archaeology (D. Ussishkin).

104 ITEM: Scarab, C(?)/0/d5; linear engraving; steatite (?), glazed white; 14.2 x 10.4 x 6.2 mm.
DECORATION: Horizontally arranged: an elaborate $sm3$-$t3.wy$, "Union of the Two Lands", flanked by symmetrically set $^c n\underline{h}$-signs, each one above a nb.
PARALLELS: Design Class 3A1.

2:1

2:1

89

DATE: Dyn. XII-XV (ca. 1950-1550 B.C.E.), probably Dyn. XII.
PROVENANCE: Area S, locus 3770 (previously 3714), level VI or VII; LB (1550-1150 B.C.E.). Field no. 42059/80.
COLLECTION: Tel Aviv University, Institute of Archaeology (D. Ussishkin).

105 ITEM: Scarab with copper (?) ring fragment, D2/0/e6, an oblique crack crosses the seal; linear engraving; steatite (?), glazed white; 13 x 10 x 6 mm.
DECORATION: Within a scroll border consisting of four round-ended interlocking Z-spiral elements, *nb* above *nfr*. It is not clear whether (1) "all good" is meant, or whether (2) the *nb* is actually a well executed but misunderstood solar disk (see above no. 91 [Kabri]).
PARALLELS: Design Classes 3, 7A1a. Petrie, BP I pls. 7:1.36 and 10:101. Tufnell, Lachish IV pl. 34/35:145. Bietak, MDAIK 23 (1968) pl. 32c (bottom, second from left) and d (lower left).
DATE: Dyn. XII-XV (ca. 1950-1550 B.C.E.), probably Dyn. XII.
PROVENANCE: Area S, locus 3612, level VI; end of LB II B (ca. 1200-1150 B.C.E.). Field no. 43565/80.
COLLECTION: Tel Aviv University, Institute of Archaeology (D. Ussishkin).

106 ITEM: Scarab, base slightly damaged; linear engraving, partial hatching; light-grey steatite, glazed white; 13.8 x 10.3 x 6.4 mm.
DECORATION: The prenomen *ᶜ3-ḫpr-n-Rᶜ*, i.e. Tuthmosis II (1482-1479 B.C.E.), in a cartouche, flanked by two *m3ᶜt*-feathers, with upended *nb* on each end.
PARALLELS: Tufnell, Lachish IV pl. 37/38:283. Petrie, BP I pl. 12:161. This is another instance indicating that pairs of *m3ᶜt*-feathers flanking royal names (with or without cartouches) would appear to be characteristic of Dyn. XVIII.
DATE: Mid-Dyn. XVIII (ca. 1482-1450 B.C.E.).
PROVENANCE: Area S, locus 3862, level VII A; earlier LB II B (ca. 1300-1200 B.C.E.). Field no. 43781/80.
COLLECTION: Tel Aviv University, Institute of Archaeology (D. Ussishkin).

107 ITEM: Scarab, C1/0/d5(?); sunk relief; white paste (?); 18.5 x 14.5 x 9 mm.
DECORATION: Within a broad rope border, an oval with two signs: the upper perhaps a seated figure, the lower a *nb*.
PARALLELS: Design Classes 3, 8A. Starkey/Harding, BP II pl. 53:208.
DATE: Dyn. XIX-XX (1292-1075 B.C.E.).
PROVENANCE: Area S, locus 3852 (pit), level VI; end of LB II B (ca. 1200-1150 B.C.E.). Field no. 44064/80.
COLLECTION: Tel Aviv University, Institute of Archaeology (D. Ussishkin).

108 ITEM: Bes figure with engraved base and pillar; head and shoulders partially lost, due to fracture; fayence; height 26 mm., base 19 x 14.5 mm.
DECORATION: Within a rectangular double line border *Ptḥ Sḫm.t nb<.t> pt*, "Ptah (and) Sakhmet the Lady of Heaven". The *ḥ* has been written with the *niwt*,

2:1

91

and the *pt* written upside down, as there was insufficient space for it beneath the *nb*. The back-pillar is also inscribed: *di ᶜnḫ nb im3 ḫw ib ḏ<t> ᶜnḫ*, "given life, (the) revered one, Ib, living forever".
DATE: Ramesside, Dyn. XIX-XX (1292-1075 B.C.E.).
PROVENANCE: Area G, locus 4077, level III; earlier Iron Age II C (ca. 750-700 B.C.E.). Field no. 10799/80.
COLLECTION: Tel Aviv University, Institute of Archaeology (D. Ussishkin).

Matzuva

(5 km. north-east of Tel Achziv; 1650/2745)

109   ITEM: Scarab, border damaged, small part missing; linear engraving; 14.5 x 9.9 x 6.5 mm.
DECORATION: Horizontally arranged: a *nwb*, flanked by two *ᶜnḫ*, above which is a group of upended anra-type signs: *3ḫt* (?), *n* (or *ḏd*?), and *ᶜ*.
PARALLELS: Design Class 3B6. Petrie, BP I pls. 7:16 and 22:227. Starkey/ Harding, BP II pl. 53:234. Hornung/Staehelin, Skarabäen Basel nos. 503 and 505. Below no. 112 (Michal).
DATE: Dyn. XII-XV (ca. 1900-1550 B.C.E.).
PROVENANCE: Surface find (?).
COLLECTION: Unknown.

Tel Michal

Excavations at Tel Michal have been conducted by the Archaeological Expedition to the Coastal Plain of Israel, headed by Dr. Z. Herzog of the Institute of Archaeology of Tel Aviv University and Prof. J. Muhly of the University of Pennsylvania, in 1977-1980. According to their preliminary conclusions, the founding of the city would have taken place probably in MB II B with the building of an earthen rampart and platform on the upper tell. However, no occupational surfaces were found for this period, nor did the excavations reach earlier strata which could remain untouched in greater depth. The site was further occupied during the LB I (16th-15th cent. B.C.E.), resettled in Iron Age I and II (11th-8th cent. B.C.E.) and resettled again, after another occupational gap of several centuries, in the Persian period (5th-4th cent. B.C.E.). In Hellenistic and Roman times and once again in the early Arab period, the tell was occupied mainly by fortress structures of military purpose.

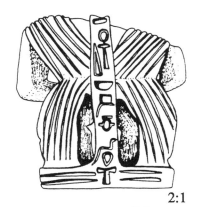

2:1

The following Egyptian-type finds (scarabs, seal impressions and amulets), which we are able to present through the courtesy of Dr. Z. Herzog, all date to the Middle or Late Bronze Age. The first item is of particular interest with regard to the settlement history of Tel Michal, as it would seem to antedate MB II B and thus attest to the existence of a settlement on the site already during the second half of the 19th cent. B.C.E.

110   ITEM: Bulla (?) (actually rather a clay ball without traces of string or the like, thus not having served as a bulla); impression of a seal with linear (?) engraving; clay; 12 x 8 mm (impression).

DECORATION: In the central column: a solar disk above $n\underline{t}r$ nfr, "the good god" (a typical royal epithet); nb $t3.wy$, "the Lord of the Two Lands", the title of the Pharaoh as sovereign of both Upper and Lower Egypt, curiously written with an inversion, $t3.wy$ preceeding nb; a pair of $m3^ct$-feathers, probably belonging to an Atef crown, adorn a cartouche with the prenomen Ny-$m3^ct$-R^c, i.e. Amenemhat III (1844-1797 B.C.E.), one of the last great rulers of Dyn. XII at a time for which Egyptian influence in the Levant is increasingly well demonstrated. The central column is flanked by two symmetrical rows of hieroglyphs including a Horus-falcon, the $\underline{h}3t$-lion, the bee of lower Egypt, the Vulture of Nekhbet, goddess of Upper Egypt, an $w\underline{d}3t$-eye, and a Red Crown, likewise symbol of Lower Egypt. This grouping of signs does not yield any sense if read in sequence, but all of them have some relevance in context with the king represented by the central column. It does therefore not seem to be necessary to look for a cryptographic interpretation (Schulman: multiple trigram of Amun, Imn-R^c $nb.i$).

Although typical of the Hyksos style, there are earlier parallels for this kind of decoration, among them several items with the cartouche of Amenemhat III (see below). The end of Dyn. XII witnessed an increase in the production of scarabs and in the selection of motifs selected for use on them. Egyptian interest in Canaan increased towards the end of Dyn. XII as a response to various threats from the North. This seal impression from Tel Michal may thus be added to the royal documents of Dyn. XII found in Palestine/Israel (see Giveon, The Impact of Egypt pp. 73-80).

PARALLELS: Design Classes 3B3a, 3B4, 11A. Newberry, Scarabs pl. 9:26. Hall, Catalogue nos. 141-142.

DATE: Late Dyn. XII (ca. 1844-1750 B.C.E.)

PROVENANCE: Locus 1, surface find. Field no. 15/1.

COLLECTION: Tel Aviv University, Institute of Archaeology (Z. Herzog).

BIBLIOGRAPHY: Schulman, Tel Aviv 5 (1978) pp. 148-151 with fig. 1 and pl. 40:2. Giveon, Tel Aviv 7 (1980) pp. 90-91 n. 1.

111   ITEM: Bulla, impression of a seal with sunk relief (?), very badly encrusted; clay; 13 x 9 mm (impression).

DECORATION: The royal name Mn-$\underline{h}pr$-R^c, i.e. Tuthmose III (1479-1426 B.C.E.), which could be read as a cryptographic writing of the divine name Imn (Amun).

No drawing available.

DATE: ?
PROVENANCE: Locus 1, surface find. Field no. 16/1.
COLLECTION: Tel Aviv University, Institute of Archaeology (Z. Herzog).
BIBLIOGRAPHY: Schulman, Tel Aviv 5 (1978) p. 151 and pl. 40:3.

112 ITEM: Scarab, D5/dec./e11, base slightly damaged; linear engraving, dense hatching; grey steatite, glazed white; 23.6 x 15.3 x 11 mm.
DECORATION: A human figure seated upon a low-backed chair, with legs in the form of an animal's (lion's?) paws. The figure has shoulder-length hair or head cloth and wears a long garment with shoulder straps. The left arm is raised, the right holds a flower bent downwards, beneath which is an ^{c}nḫ. Beneath the chair is a nb. The back of the scarab is decorated with two well executed crossed branches.
PARALLELS: Design Class 10B. Macalister, Gezer III pl. 202a:7 (= StSc II: frontispiece no. 3). Tufnell, Lachish IV pl. 30/31:64. Pieper, ZDPV 53 (1930) p. 196 with pl. 9:22668. See Keel/Schroer, Stempelsiegel I pp. 84-88.
DATE: Hyksos, Dyn. XV (ca. 1650-1550 B.C.E.).
PROVENANCE: Area A, locus 965, level XVI/XV; LB I-II (1550-1150 B.C.E.). Field no. 9809/80.
COLLECTION: Tel Aviv University, Institute of Archaeology (Z. Herzog).
BIBLIOGRAPHY: Herzog et al., Tel Aviv 7/3-4 (1980) cover.

113 ITEM: Two incomplete impressions (a complete version has been restored) of an oval seal with linear engraving, partially hatched; clay; ca. 13.5 x 9 mm.
DECORATION: Horizontally arranged: an object, which may perhaps be construed as a nwb, flanked by two very stylized objects which could represent Red Crowns. Above these are three signs: a human face (? ḥr) or an unsuccessful, compressed and inverted nfr (?), between two loops, perhaps mere cord loops.
PARALLELS: Design Class 3B6.
DATE: Probably Hyksos, Dyn. XV (ca. 1650-1550 B.C.E.).
PROVENANCE: Locus 1, surface find. Field no. 12/1.
COLLECTION: Tel Aviv University, Institute of Archaeology (Z. Herzog).

114 ITEM: Scarab, B7(?)/0/d5, slightly abraded; linear engraving, scratched hatching; grey steatite, glazed white; 19.4 x 13.4 x 8.7 mm.
DECORATION: Horizontally arranged: a nwb set below three ḫpr-beetles.
PARALLELS: Design Class 3B6. Kenyon, Jericho II fig. 298:8. Hornung/ Staehelin, Skarabäen Basel no. 196.
DATE: Hyksos, Dyn. XV (ca. 1650-1550 B.C.E.).
PROVENANCE: Area A, locus 882, level XVI; LB I (1550-1400 B.C.E.). Field no. 5787/80.
COLLECTION: Tel Aviv University, Institute of Archaeology (Z. Herzog).

2:1

  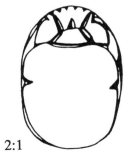

2:1

115 ITEM: Scarab, D1/0/e10, slightly abraded (?); linear engraving; steatite; 17 x 11.4 x 6.5 mm.
DECORATION: Horizontally arranged: a *nwb* flanked by two *nfr* below a series of upended anra type hieroglyphs (*r, n, ᶜ, ḫᶜ*) without any apparent significance.
PARALLELS: Design Class 3B6. Petrie, AG V pl. 9:79. Macalister, Gezer III pl. 203b:12 (= Rowe, Catalogue no. 222). See above no. 109 (Matzuva).
DATE: Dyn. XIII (ca. 1750-1650 B.C.E.).
PROVENANCE: Area A, locus 983, level XVI/XV; LB I-II (1550-1150 B.C.E.). Field no. 9801/80.
COLLECTION: Tel Aviv University, Institute of Archaeology (Z. Herzog).

116 ITEM: Scarab, border abraded; partially sunk relief, partially linear engraving; steatite, glazed white; 11.3 x 8.8 x 6.2 mm.
DECORATION: Horizontally arranged: tilapia fish with a two-blossomed plant in its mouth and a lotus bud behind its tail fin. This fish was significant as it was associated with regenerative powers by the ancient Egyptians, as was the lotus.
PARALLELS: Hornung/Staehelin, Skarabäen Basel no. B 17. Petrie, AG I pl. 14:137 (= Rowe, Catalogue no. 597).
DATE: Dyn. XVIII - mid-Dyn. XX (ca. 1550-1150 B.C.E.).
PROVENANCE: Area A, locus 1653, level XV; LB II (1400-1150 B.C.E.). Field no. 10449/80.
COLLECTION: Tel Aviv University, Institute of Archaeology (Z. Herzog).

117 ITEM: Scarab, D8/0/e10, somewhat battered; linear engraving; steatite, glazed white; 20.3 x 10.4 x 8.8 mm.
DECORATION: A convoluted coiled pattern within a rope border.
PARALLELS: Design Classes 6B1, 8A.
DATE: Hyksos, Dyn. XV (ca. 1650-1550 B.C.E.).
PROVENANCE: Area A, locus 1702, stratum XV; LB II (1400-1150 B.C.E.). Field no. 10722/80.
COLLECTION: Tel Aviv University, Institute of Archaeology (Z. Herzog).

118 ITEM: Fragment of statuette of Mut; fayence; 48 x 24 mm.
The head, wig and part of the double crown (with broken uraeus) are preserved. On the dorsal column is a corrupt inscription with introductory words of religious nature: *mdw ḏd n Mwt*, "words to be spoken (or recited) by (the Theban goddess) Mut:...". *Mwt* means "mother" as well as being the name of the goddess; this explains her presence on an amulet. Similar fayence objects were distributed not only along the Levantine Coast (cf., e.g., Rowe, Catalogue no. A. 21), but throughout the Mediterranean basin by the Phoenicians (cf., e.g., Popham/Sackett, Lefkandi I pls. 178 and 233:e. Gamer-Wallert, Iberische Halbinsel pls. 35-47 and 54).
DATE: LB II B - Iron Age II B (1300-800 B.C.E.).

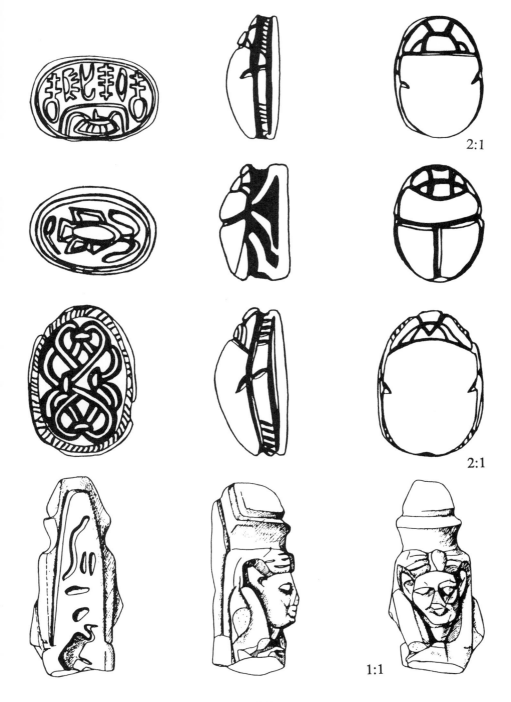

2:1

2:1

1:1

99

PROVENANCE: Locus 2, surface find. Field no. 25/80.
COLLECTION: Tel Aviv University, Institute of Archaeology (Z. Herzog).

119   ITEM: Fragment of an amulet in the form of an $w\underline{d}3t$-eye, partially restored; fayence; broken, not measurable.
PROVENANCE: Area E, locus 1858, tomb, strata VIII/VI; Persian period. Field no. 11630/80.
COLLECTION: Tel Aviv University, Institute of Archaeology (Z. Herzog).
NOTE: Two additional $w\underline{d}3t$-eye amulets, both made of mother-of-pearl, one complete and one broken, were found in the Persian period cemetery of Tel Michal and will be published together with the beads in the final excavation report.

Sa^car

(Kibbutz at the northeastern edge of Nahariya; 1605/2705)

120   ITEM: Scarab, base somewhat damaged; stone; measurements?
DECORATION: Horizontally arranged: a falcon-headed griffin couchant, whose two wings are vertically spread, with the head in profile and turned backwards. The tail is standing jauntily in the air. Above the griffin's head, a drill hole may be taken as representing a sun disk.
PARALLELS: Giveon, Footsteps of Pharaoh in Canaan, Tel Aviv 1984, p. 148 (hebr.). Vollenweider, Genève nos. 158-159. Hornung/Staehelin, Skarabäen Basel no. 645. Gamer-Wallert, Iberische Halbinsel no. B 25. Matz, CMS I pp. 318:282, 330:293, 392:383, 395:389. The original Aegean influence seems to be notably clear, but early parallels are rare. It is not clear however whether an older seal or ivory inspired this work in the first millennium or whether it is actually contemporaneous with the explicit parallels.
DATE: LB II - Iron Age II (1400-586 B.C.E.).
PROVENANCE: Surface find (Amir Shapir), plantation of the Kibbutz Sa^car.
COLLECTION: Amir Shapir, Kibbutz Ḥanita.

Tel Shem

(arabic Tell Shamam, 1 km. south-south-east of Moshav Kefar Yehoshua^c in the Yezreel plain; 1647/2307)

121   ITEM: Scarab; sunk relief; serpentine, speckled; 19 x 13 x 8 mm.
DECORATION: At the top, the prenomen $Wsr\text{-}m3^ct\text{-}R^c$, i.e. Ramesses II (1279-1213 B.C.E.), below this the epithet $stp\text{-}<n>\text{-}R^c$, "selected by Re". Thoth (with full and crescent moons upon his head), the ibis-headed divinity responsible for the moon and graphics, holds a $w3s$-sceptre. Behind him is a mr which allows for the reading $mry\ \underline{D}hwty$, "(Ramesses II) beloved of Thoth".

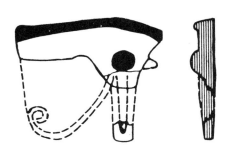

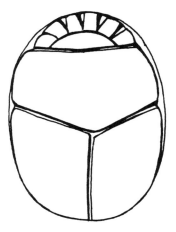

PARALLELS: If no exact parallels are known to us, it is nevertheless possible to interpret the decoration of this scarab as a conflation of two different types: first, the association of the prenomen $Wsr-m3^ct-R^c$ with the epithet *mry Ḏḥwty* (where, however, the god is usually represented as a sitting baboon; cf. Hornung/ Staehelin, Skarabäen Basel no. 401 with parallels); second, the writing of the prenomen of Remesses II with a figure of the standing sun-god with *w3s*-sceptre instead of a simple sun-disk (cf. Hall, Catalogue nos. 2170-2178). Cf. also Giveon/Kertesz, Acco no. 53; Starkey/Harding, BP II pl. 57:373 = Rowe, Catalogue no. 665; and, for a figural representation of Thoth stylistically related to ours, ibid. no. 910 (Atlit).
DATE: Dyn. XIX-XX (ca. 1279-1070 B.C.E.).
PROVENANCE: Surface find.
COLLECTION: Beit Hankin Museum, IDAM No. 80-803.

Tel Yitzḥaqi

(arabic Khirbet esh-Sheikh Iskhaqiya near Kefar Yehoshua[c]
at the north-western end of the Yezreel plain; 162/232)

Queen Hatshepsut has already been found attested on scarabs from Beth Shean and Jericho. It is strange to find this piece in a less significant place.

122   ITEM: Scarab, side slightly damaged; sunk relief, partially hatched; steatite; 18.9 x 13.5 x 8.6 mm.
DECORATION: The prenomen $M3^ct-k3-R^c$, i.e. Hatshepsut (1479-1457 B.C.E.), with the epithet *nb[.t] t3.wy ḥq3[.t]*, "Lord of the Two Lands and Ruler (par excellence)", with the *nb* upside down. The last sign has been interpreted as representing a combined *nb* and feminine *t*-ending for *ḥq3.t* (Leclant). The royal name is not enclosed within a cartouche.
PARALLELS: While *ḥq3-t3.wy* is already recorded on scarabs under Ahmose (see Hornung/Staehelin, Skarabäen Basel p. 56), the use of *ḥq3* followed by the two land signs seems then to be generally restricted to various verb forms, in contradistinction to its use in conjunction with the two plants symbolizing Upper and Lower Egypt (cf. Urk. IV 378,1 and 577,17). For parallels see Matouk, Corpus I p. 209:244-245. Rowe, Catalogue nos. 471 (Beth Shean) and 472 (Jericho).
DATE: Dyn. XVIII, Hatshepsut (1479-1457 B.C.E.). Due to the contempt to which Hatshepsut was subjected after her departure from power, it is improbable that the piece should be dated to any period other than that of her reign, a proposition which is reinforced by the quality and type of work on its back.
PROVENANCE: No stratified context; surface find (?).
COLLECTION: Jerusalem, IDAM 76-5015.
BIBLIOGRAPHY: Leclant, Or. N.S. 45 (1976) p. 310.

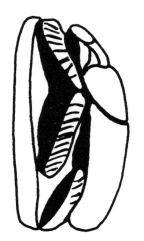

103

Abbreviations

for periodicals, series and reference works cited

AG	PETRIE et al., Ancient Gaza*
AJBA	Australian Journal of Biblical Archaeology
AnSt	Anatolian Studies
ASAE	Annales du Service des Antiquités de l'Egypte
BASOR	Bulletin of the American Schools of Oriental Research
BDS	PETRIE, Buttons and Design Scarabs*
BIES	Bulletin of the Israel Exploration Society
BiOr	Bibliotheca Orientalis
BN	Biblische Notizen
BP	PETRIE et al., Beth-Pelet*
BSFE	Bulletin de la Société Francaise d'Egyptologie
CG	NEWBERRY, Catalogue général*
ChdE	Chronique d'Egypte
EA	KNUDTZON, Die El-Amarna-Tafeln*
GM	Göttinger Miszellen
IEJ	Israel Exploration Journal
JARCE	Journal of the American Research Center in Egypt
JBL	Journal of Biblical Literature
JEA	Journal of Egyptian Archaeology
JJS	Journal of Jewish Studies
JNES	Journal of Near Eastern Studies
MDAIK	Mitteilungen des Deutschen Archäologischen Instituts, Abteilung Kairo
Or.N.S.	Orientalia
PEQ	Palestine Exploration Quarterly
PN	RANKE, Die ägyptischen Personennamen*
PSBA	Proceedings of the Society for Biblical Archaeology
RB	Revue Biblique
RdE	Revue d'Egyptologie
RSO	Rivista degli Studi Orientali
SAK	Studien zur altägyptischen Kultur
SCN	PETRIE, Scarabs and Cylinders with Names*
StSc	TUFNELL/WARD, Studies on Scarab Seals*
UF	Ugarit Forschungen
VT	Vetus Testamentum
Wb.	ERMAN/GRAPOW, Wörterbuch der ägyptischen Sprache*
ZÄS	Zeitschrift für ägyptische Sprache und Altertumskunde
ZDPV	Zeitschrift des Deutschen Palästina-Vereins

* See bibliography of reference works cited below.

Reference Works

and articles cited in the catalogue

ALP S., Zylinder- und Stempelsiegel aus Karahöyük bei Konya, Ankara 1968.

ANATI E., Hazorea: IEJ 21 (1971) pp. 172-173.

— Abu Zureiq (Hazorea): RB 78 (1971) pp. 582-584.

ANTHES R. et al., Mit Rahineh 1955 (University Museum Monographs), Philadelphia 1959.

BIETAK M., Vorläufiger Bericht über die erste und zweite Kampagne der österreichischen Ausgrabungen auf Tell Ed-Dab^{c}a im Ostdelta Ägyptens (1966, 1967): MDAIK 23 (1968) pp. 79-114.

— Vorläufiger Bericht über die dritte Kampagne der österreichischen Ausgrabungen auf Tell Ed-Dab^{c}a im Ostdelta Ägyptens (1968): MDAIK 26 (1970) pp. 15-42.

BRUNNER-TRAUT E., Spitzmaus und Ichneumon als Tiere des Sonnengottes. Nachrichten der Akademie der Wissenschaften in Göttingen, 1965, No. 7, pp. 123-163.

BRUYERE B., Rapport sur les Fouilles de Deir el-Médineh, 15 vols., Le Caire 1924-1953.

BUHL M.-L./HOLM-NIELSEN S., Shiloh: The Danish Excavations (Publications of the Danish National Museum. Archaeological-Historical Series 12), Copenhagen 1969.

COLDSTREAM J. N., Greeks and Phoenicians in the Aegean, in: H. G. NIEMEYER (ed.), Phönizier im Westen = Madrider Beiträge 8 (1982) pp. 261-275.

DARESSY G., Statue de Zedher le Sauveur: ASAE 18 (1918) pp. 113-158.

DRIOTON E., Pages d'Egyptologie, Le Caire 1957.

DUNBABIN T.J. et al., Perachora. The Sanctuaries of Hera Akraia and Limenia. Excavations of the British School of Archaeology at Athens, 1930-1933. Vol. II: Pottery, Ivories, Scarabs, and Other Objects from the Votive Deposit of Hera Limenia, Oxford 1962.

ERMAN A./GRAPOW H. (eds.), Wörterbuch der ägyptischen Sprache, 7 vols., Berlin, 1926-1953 [= Wb.].

GALLING K., Die Kopfzier der Philister in den Darstellungen von Medinet Habu, in: Ugaritica VI (Mission de Ras Shamra XVII = Bibliothèque archéologique et historique LXXXI), Paris 1969, pp. 247-265.

GAMER-WALLERT I., Ägyptische und ägyptisierende Funde von der Iberischen Halbinsel (Tübinger Atlas zum Vorderen Orient. Beiheft Reihe B Nr. 21), Wiesbaden 1978.

GARDINER A. H., Egyptian Grammar, Oxford ^{3}1957.

GIVEON R., Egyptian Seals from Kefar Ruppin: BIES 25 (1961) pp. 249-250 (hebr.).

105

---   The Impact of Egypt on Canaan. Iconographical and Related Studies (Orbis Biblicus et Orientalis 20), Fribourg/Switzerland and Göttingen 1978.

---   Fouilles et Travaux de l'Université de Tel-Aviv. Découvertes égyptiennes récentes: BSFE 81 (1978) pp. 6-17.

---   Some Scarabs from Canaan with Egyptian Titles: Tel Aviv 7 (1980) pp. 179-184.

---   Egyptian Scarabs from Western Asia from the Collections of the British Museum (Orbis Biblicus et Orientalis. Series Archaeologica 3), Fribourg/Switzerland and Göttingen 1985.

---   /KERTESZ T., Egyptian Scarabs and Seals from Acco. From the Collection of the Israel Department of Antiquities and Museums, Fribourg/Switzerland 1986.

GJERSTAD E. et al., The Swedish Cyprus Expedition. Finds and Results of the Excavations in Cyprus 1927-1931, 4 vols., Stockholm 1934-1972.

GRANT E., Rumeileh. Being Ain Shems Excavations (Palestine) vol. III (Biblical and Kindred Studies 5), Haverford 1934.

HALL H. R., Catalogue of Egyptian Scarabs, Etc., in the British Museum. Vol. I: Royal Scarabs, London 1913.

HAYES W. C., Inscriptions from the Palace of Amenhotep III: JNES 10 (1951) pp. 35-56.82-112.156-183.231-242.

HAYES W. C., The Scepter of Egypt, 2 vols., New York 1953 + 1959.

HERZOG Z. et al., Excavations at Tel Michal 1978-1979: Tel Aviv 7/3-4 (1980) pp. 111-151.

---   /RAPP G./NEGBI O., Excavations at Tel Michal, Israel, Minnesota and Tel Aviv 1987.

HÖLBL G., Typologische Arbeit bei der Interpretation von nicht klar lesbaren Skarabäenflachseiten: SAK 7 (1979) pp. 89-102.

---   Beziehungen der ägyptischen Kultur zu Altitalien (Etudes préliminaires aux religions orientales dans l'empire romain 62), 2 vols., Leiden 1979.

HORNUNG E./STAEHELIN E., Skarabäen und andere Siegelamulette aus Basler Sammlungen (Ägyptische Denkmäler in der Schweiz 1), Basel 1976.

JAEGER B., Essai de classification et datation des scarabées Menkhéperrê (Orbis Biblicus et Orientalis. Series Archaeologica 2), Fribourg/Switzerland and Göttingen 1982.

JOHNS C. N., Excavations at ᶜAtlit (1930-1931). The South-eastern Cemetery: QDAP 2 (1933) pp. 41-104.

KEEL O., Der Bogen als Herrschaftssymbol. Einige unveröffentlichte Skarabäen aus Ägypten und Israel zum Thema "Jagd und Krieg": ZDPV 93 (1977) pp. 141-177.

--- Jahwe-Visionen und Siegelkunst. Eine neue Deutung der Majestätsschilderungen in Jes 6, Ez 1 und 10 und Sach 4 (Stuttgarter Bibelstudien 84/85), Stuttgart 1977.

--- La Glyptique, in: J. BRIEND/J.-B. HUMBERT (eds.), Tell Keisan (1971-1976). Une cité phénicienne en Galilée (Orbis Biblicus et Orientalis. Series Archaeologica 1), Fribourg/Switzerland and Göttingen 1980, pp. 257-295.

KENYON K.M., Excavations at Jericho, 2 vols., London 1960 + 1965.

KNUDTZON J. A. et al., Die el-Amarna Tafeln mit Einleitung und Erklärungen (Vorderasiatische Bibliothek 2), 2 vols., Leipzig 1915 (Reprint Aalen 1964) [= EA].

KOCHAVI M., Aphek-Antipatris. Five Seasons of Excavation at Tel Aphek-Antipatris (1972-1976), Tel Aviv 1977.

LAMON R. S., The Megiddo Water System (Oriental Institute Publications 32), Chicago 1935.

LAMON R.S./SHIPTON G.M., Megiddo I. Seasons of 1925-1934, Strata I-V (Oriental Institute Publications 42), Chicago 1939.

LECLANT J., Fouilles et travaux en Egypte et au Soudan, 1974-1975: Or. N.S. 45 (1976) pp. 275-318.

--- et al., Scarabées, amulettes et figurines, in: G. CLERC et al., Fouilles de Kition. Vol. II: Objets égyptiens et égyptisants, Nicosia 1976, pp. 19-165.

--- Fouilles et travaux en Egypte et au Soudan, 1980-1981: Or. N.S. 51 (1982) pp. 411-492.

LOUD G., The Megiddo Ivories (Oriental Institute Publications 52), Chicago 1939.

--- et al., Megiddo II. Seasons of 1935-1939 (Oriental Institute Publications 62), 2 vols., Chicago 1948.

MACALISTER R.A.S., The Excavation of Gezer. 1902-1905 and 1907-1909, 3 vols., London 1912.

MARKOE G., Phoenician Bronze and Silver Bowls from Cyprus and the Mediterranean (University of California Publications. Classical Studies 26), Berkeley-Los Angeles-London 1985.

MATOUK F.S., Corpus du Scarabée Egyptien. Vol. I: Les scarabées royaux. Vol. II: Analyse thématique, Beyrouth n. d. [1971+1977].

MATTHIAE SCANDONE G., Scarabei e scaraboidi egiziani ed egittizanti del Museo Nazionale di Cagliari (Collezione di studi fenici 7), Rome 1975.

MATZ F. et al. (eds.), Corpus der minoischen und mykenischen Siegel, 13 vols. + 2 suppl. vols., Berlin 1964-1974.

MAYER-OPIFICIUS R., Die geflügelte Sonne. Himmels- und Regendarstellungen im Alten Orient: UF 16 (1984) pp. 189-236.

MURRAY A. S. et al., Excavations in Cyprus, London 1900.

107

NEWBERRY P. E., Scarabs, London 1908.

— Catalogue général des antiquités égyptiennes du Musée du Caire. Nos. 36001-37521: Scarab-shaped Seals, London 1907 [= CG].

— The Timins Collection of Ancient Egyptian Scarabs and Cylinder Seals, London 1907.

PETRIE W. M. F. et al., Naukratis. Part I: 1884-5 (Memoir of the Egypt Exploration Fund), London 1886.

— Hyksos and Israelite Cities (British School of Archaeology in Egypt 12), London 1906.

— /WALKER J.H., Memphis I (British School of Archaeology in Egypt 15), London 1909.

— Scarabs and Cylinders with Names. Illustrated by the Egyptian Collection in University College, London (British School of Archaeology in Egypt 21), London 1917 (Reprint Warminster-Encino/Cal. 1974) [= SCN].

— Buttons and Design Scarabs. Illustrated by the Egyptian Collection in University College, London (British School of Archaeology in Egypt 24), London 1925 (Reprint Warminster-Encino/Cal. 1974) [= BDS].

— Gerar (British School of Archaeology in Egypt 43), London 1928.

— et al., Beth Pelet I (Tell Fara) (British School of Archaeology 48), London 1930 [= BP I].

— et al., Ancient Gaza (Tell el-Ajjul), 5 vols. (British School of Archaeology in Egypt 53-56 + 64), London 1931-1952 [= AG].

PIEPER M., Die Bedeutung der Skarabäen für die palästinensische Altertumskunde: ZDPV 53 (1930) 185-199.

POPHAM M.R./SACKETT L.H., Lefkandi I (British School of Archaeology at Athens. Supplementary Volume 11), London 1980.

PRITCHARD J., The Bronze Age Cemetery at Gibeon (University Museum Monographs 4), Philadelphia 1963.

RANKE H., Die ägyptischen Personennamen. Bd. I: Verzeichnis der Namen. Bd. II: Inhalt und Geschichte der Namen. Bd. III: Verzeichnisse der Bestandteile, Glückstadt 1935 + 1952 + 1977 [= PN].

ROWE A., A Catalogue of Egyptian Scarabs, Scaraboids, Seals and Amulets in the Palestine Archaeological Museum, Le Caire 1936.

SCHACHERMEYR F., Hörnerhelme und Federkrone als Kopfbedeckungen bei den "Seevölkern" der ägyptischen Reliefs, in: Ugaritica VI (Mission de Ras Shamra XVII = Bibliothèque archéologique et historique LXXXI), Paris 1969, pp. 451-459.

SCHUHMACHER G., Tell el-Mutesellim I, 2 vols., Berlin 1908.

SCHULMAN A. R., Two Scarab Impressions from Tel Michal: Tel Aviv 5 (1978) pp. 148-151.

SETHE K., Atum als Ichneumon: ZÄS 63 (1928) pp. 50-53.

SLIWA J., Egyptian Scarabs, scaraboids and plaques from the Cracow Collections (Studia ad Archaeologiam Mediteraneam pertinentia 8), Cracow 1985.

STAEHELIN E., Ägyptens heilige Pillendreher. Von Skarabäen und anderen Siegelamuletten, Basel 1982.

STARKEY J.L./HARDING L./MACDONALD E., Beth-Pelet II. Prehistoric Fara. Beth-Pelet Cemetery (British School of Archaeology in Egypt 52), London 1932 [= BP II].

TUFNELL O., Lachish III (Tel ed-Duweir). The Iron Age, 2 vols., London etc. 1953.

---   et al., Lachish IV (Tel ed-Duweir). The Bronze Age, 2 vols., London etc. 1958.

---   Studies on Scarab Seals. Vol. II: Scarab Seals and their Contribution to History in the Early Second Millennium B.C. With Contributions by G.T. MARTIN and W.A. WARD, 2 vols., Warminster 1984 [= StSc II].

USSISHKIN D., Excavations at Tel Lachish 1973-1977: Tel Aviv 5 (1978) pp. 1-97.

VERCOUTTER J., Les objets égyptiens et égyptisants du mobilier funéraire carthaginois (Bibliothèque archéologique et historique 40), Paris 1945.

VODOZ I., Catalogue raisonné des scarabées gravés du Musée d'art et d'histoire de Genève (Aegyptiaca Helvetica), Genève 1979.

VOLLENWEIDER M.-L., Catalogue raisonné des sceaux cylindres et intailles. Vol. I, Genève 1967.

WAINWRIGHT G. A., Balabish (Egypt Exploration Society. Memoir 27), London 1920.

WARD J., A Collection of Historical Scarabs and Others, with a few Cylinders: PSBA 22 (1900) pp. 305-320.386-401; 23 (1901) pp. 19-34.79-91.

WARD W.A., The Origin of Egyptian Design-Amulets (Button-Seals): JEA 56 (1970) pp. 65-80.

---   Studies on Scarab Seals. Vol. I: Pre-12th Dynasty Scarab Amulets. With an Appendix on the Biology of Scarab Beetles by S.I. BISHARA, Warminster 1978 [= StSc I].

WEIPPERT H., Siegel mit Mondsichelstandarten aus Palästina: BN 5 (1978) pp. 43-58.

Index

Motif Index

Amun-Trigrams and cryptographic
writings *6?, 17?, 24, 25?, 62,*
73, 74?, 92, 110?, 111?

Animals

Bird *57, 60, 62*

Crocodile *42, 47, 73*

Donkey *25*

Fish *116*

Goose *62*

Hippopotamus *38?*

Horse *77*

Ibex *1, 30, 38, 45, 76*

Ichneumon *6, ?*

Lion *1, 28, 58, 68, 73, 94*

Celestial

Crescent Moon *61, 121*

Horizon *7*

Solar Barque *93*

Solar Disk *9, 6, 14, 15, 17,*
26, 91, 93, 110

Circles *33, 36*

Cross, Coil and Spiral Patterns *7,*
8, 10, 27, 32, 35, 36, 48, 51,
54, 56, 69, 72, 74, 79, 83,
102, 105, 117

Crowns

Atef Crown *102, 110*

Blue Crown *21, 94, 102*

Double Crown *19, 21, 118*

Red Crown *25, 39, 58, 78,*
96, 97?, 101, 110, 113

Divine Animals

Donkey *25, 94*

Falcon *20, 64, 66, 99, 110*

Goose *62*

Griffon *16, 76, 78, 120*

Ichneumon *6, 17*

Sphinx *19, 21, 59, 102*

Uraeus *21, 30, 42, 52, 66,*
70?, 73, 78, 80, 93, 97

Divinities

Amun *24, 25, 98*

Amun-Re^c *46, 92, 75*

Anubis *97?*

Bes *22, 108*

Falcon-headed god *23, 31, 42;*
see Horus, Re^c-Harakhte

Horus *64, 99, 110;* see
Falcon-headed god, Re^c-
Harakhte

Khonsu *5, 98*

Maat *15*

Mut *118*

Naked goddess *44*

Nekhbet *14?, 110*

Onuris *12?*

Ptah *98*

Re^c *6, 15*

Re^c-Atum *6?, 17?*

Re^c-Harakhte *31,* see Falcon-
headed god

Sakhmet *64*

111

Seth 25, 94, 97?

Thoth 121

Triad 98

Egyptian Hieroglyphs, Words and
Phrases

3ḫt-horizon (N27) 7, 19?

i-reed (M17) 3, 23, 28, 92, 73

iwn-column (O28) 6, 17

imy-r-pr "Steward" 37, 81

ᶜ-arm (D42) 30

ᶜ3-nṯr, "the great god" 20

ᶜnḫ -sign, "life" (S34) 3, 4,
43, 57, 59, 60, 65, 82, 104,
110

anra-type sign groups 29, 82,
110, 115

ᶜd-netting (V26) 30

w3ḫ-swab (V29) 65

w3s-sceptre (S40) 31, 42, 55?,
121

w3ḏ-papyrus (M13) 41, 59,
65, 82

wᶜ-harpoon (T21) 33

wḏ3t-eye (D10) 55, 65, 97,
110, 119; cf. 13

pt-sky (N1) 98

m-owl (G17) 5, 25

m3ᶜt-feather, "truth justice"
(H6) 24, 31, 40, 73, 92, 93,
106, 110

mn-board (Y5) 19, 26, 29

mry-Ḏhwty, "beloved of Thoth"
121

mḫ-whip (V22) 30

mdw-ḏd-n-Mwt, "Words spoken
by Mut" 118

n-water-line (N35) 29, 62, 77,
97, 110?

niwt-city-determinative (O49)
108

nb-basket, "lord" (V30)
passim

nb-t3.wy, "Lord of the Two
Lands" 59?, 65, 110

nwb-collar, "gold" (S12) 10,
43, 67, 113, 114, 115, 91

nfr "good" (F35) 7, 24, 39,
43, 56, 78, 94, 105, 113?, 115

nmt.t nb.t n ip.t, "(My) every
stride belongs to the harem (of
Amun, i.e. Luxor)" 11

nḥm, "saviour" 92

nsw-bity, "King of Upper and
Lower Egypt" 43, 55; see 110

nṯr, "god" (R8) 20, 21, 78, 81

nṯr-nfr, "good (or perfect) god"
53?, 74, 110

nṯr-ᶜnḫ, "(the) living god" 26

r-mouth (D21) 30, 37

Rᶜ nfr, "the good (sun-god)
Reᶜ" 94

ḫ3-plant (M16) 60

ḫ3t-lion (F4) 110

ḥb-festival-sign (W3)

ḥm-club, "servant" or "majesty"
(U36) 39, 59, 81, 114

ḥr-face(D2) 113?

ḥsy-m3ᶜt-Rᶜ, "praised is the
justice of Reᶜ" 15

ḥsy-nb-t3.wy, "he whom the
Lord of the Two Lands praises"
59?

ḥk3-t3.wy, "Ruler of the Two
Lands" 65

112

ḥtp-altar, "offering" or "peace"
(R4) *81*

ḫ^c-hill, "appearance" (N28)
29, 115

ḫpr-bettle (L1) *55, 114*

ḫpr.w-ḫ^c.w, "Manifestations of
the Diadems (or Weapons, or
Appearances)" *99*

Ḫnsw m s3<.y> "Khonsu is
<my> protection" *5*

ḫrw-oar (P8) *57*

s3-papyrus (V17), "protection"
5

s3w-guardian (A48),
"protection" *63*

sw-plant (M23) *57, 60?*; see
nsw-bity

sm3-t3.wy, "Union of the Two
Lands" (F36 and N16) *104*

šn-ring, symbol of rulership
(V9) *19, 59*

k3-arms, "double" or "soul"
(D28) *55, 78*

t3-sign, "land" (N16) *39?, 92*

di-^cnḫ, "given life" *98*

ḏd-column, "stability" (R11)
39, 55, 110?

Floral Elements *2, 3, 9, 35, 36,
42, 44, 45, 47, 51, 59, 62, 64,
80, 92, 94, 101, 113, 116*

Griffin *16, 76, 78, 120*

Hippopotami *38?*

Human Figures *2, 3, 4, 12, 22,
42, 44, 47, 52, 77, 79, 98,
107?, 112*

Ibex *1, 30, 38, 76*

Maltese cross *48*

Pharaoh *94, 102*

Prisoners *22, 101*

Rosette (see also "Coiled", etc.)
10, 27, 35

Royal names
   ^c3-ḫpr-n-R^c - Tuthmose II *106*

   Wsr-m3^ct-R^c - Ramesses II
   18, 53, 70, 121

   M3^ct-k3-R^c - Hatshepsut *65*

   Mn-m3^ct-R^c - Seti I *64*

   Mn-ḫpr-R^c - Tuthmose III *20,
   64, 74, 99, 111*; cf. *13*

   Mn-k3[.w]-R^c - Mykerinos *64*

   Ny-m3^ct-R^c - Amenemhat III
   110

   Nb-pḥty-R^c - Ahmose *9*

   Nb-m3^ct-R^c - Amenophis III
   49, 50

   R^c-mss - Ramesses (I?) *40*

"Sacred trees" *16*

Sphinx
   see Divine Animals

Uraeus
   see Divine Animals

Winged (sun-)disk *7?, 14*

Tufnell/Ward
Design Classes

Design Class 1 *2, 35, 38, 44, 67, 100*

Design Class 2 *34, 41, 51, 54, 56, 67, 69, 91*

Design Class 3 *4, 29, 39, 43, 51, 53, 55, 56, 65, 67, 71, 81, 82, 84, 91, 95, 97, 104, 105, 107, 109,110, 113, 114, 115*

Design Class 4 *33, 36*

Design Class 5 *10, 35*

Design Class 6 *32, 72, 83, 117*

Design Class 7 *29, 33, 79, 105*

Design Class 8 *33, 71, 107, 117*

Design Class 9 *1, 30, 38, 42, 45, 47, 65, 66, 78*

Design Class 10 *2, 3, 4, 42, 44, 47, 52, 79, 112*

Design Class 11 *37, 110*

Materials Index

Amethyst *76*

Bone *19*

Carnelian *11, Aphek 29*

Clay (impressions) *39*

Fayence *50, 60?, 74, 79, 82, 98, 118, 119*

Frit *91*

Jasper *2, 4*

Limestone *61*

Paste *60?, 109*

Quartz *Aphek 30*

Serpentine *121*

Steatite *passim*

Stone *57, 120*

Seal Impressions *18, 39, 93, 101, 102, 110, 113*

114

PLATES

PLATE I

PLATE II

19   20   21   22

23   24   25   26

27   28   29   30

31   32   33

34

PLATE III

35

36

37

38

40

41

43

42

39

PLATE IV

44   45   46   47

48

51

49   50   52   53

54   55   56   57

PLATE V

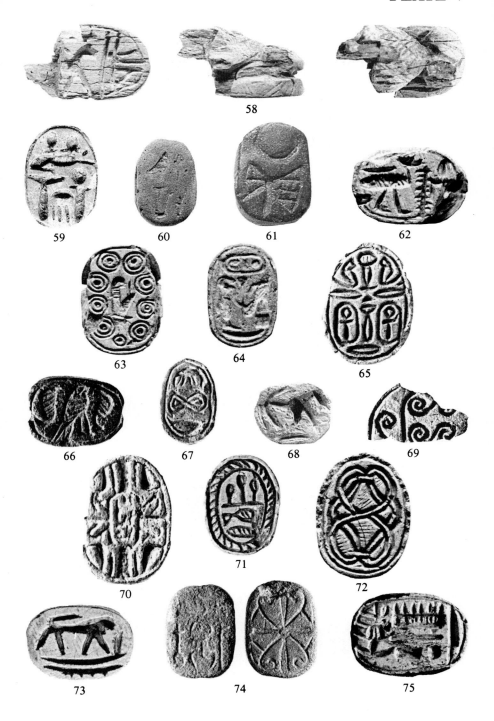

58

59   60   61   62

63   64   65

66   67   68   69

70   71   72

73   74   75

PLATE VI

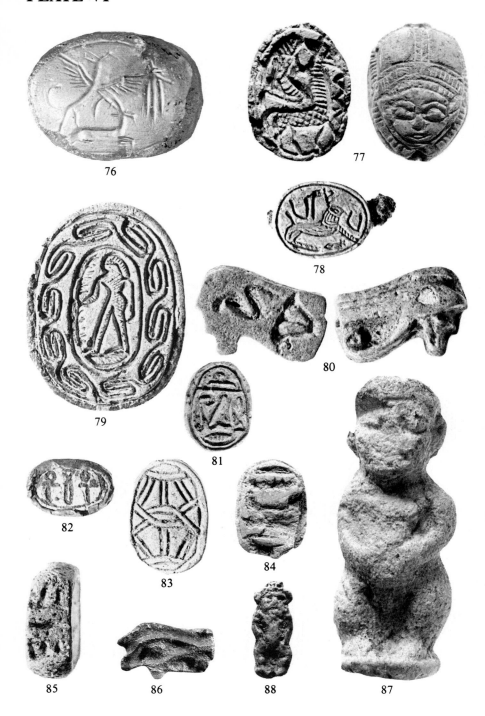

76

77

78

79

80

81

82

83

84

85

86

88

87

PLATE VII

89   90   91   93

92   94   95   96

97   98   99   101

100

102   103   104   105

PLATE VIII

106

107

108

109

110

112

113

111

115

114

116

117

PLATE IX

118

120

119

121 (impression)

122

ORBIS BIBLICUS ET ORIENTALIS

Bd. 1   OTTO RICKENBACHER: *Weisheitsperikopen bei Ben Sira.* X–214–15* Seiten. 1973. Vergriffen.

Bd. 2   FRANZ SCHNIDER: *Jesus der Prophet.* 298 Seiten. 1973. Vergriffen.

Bd. 3   PAUL ZINGG: *Das Wachsen der Kirche.* Beiträge zur Frage der lukanischen Redaktion und Theologie. 345 Seiten. 1974. Vergriffen.

Bd. 4   KARL JAROŠ: *Die Stellung des Elohisten zur kanaanäischen Religion.* 294 Seiten, 12 Abbildungen. 1982. 2. verbesserte und überarbeitete Auflage.

Bd. 5   OTHMAR KEEL: *Wirkmächtige Siegeszeichen im Alten Testament.* Ikonographische Studien zu Jos 8, 18–26; Ex 17, 8–13; 2 Kön 13, 14–19 und 1 Kön 22, 11. 232 Seiten, 78 Abbildungen. 1974. Vergriffen.

Bd. 6   VITUS HUONDER: *Israel Sohn Gottes.* Zur Deutung eines alttestamentlichen Themas in der jüdischen Exegese des Mittelalters. 231 Seiten. 1975.

Bd. 7   RAINER SCHMITT: *Exodus und Passa.* Ihr Zusammenhang im Alten Testament. 124 Seiten. 1982. 2. neubearbeitete Auflage.

Bd. 8   ADRIAN SCHENKER: *Hexaplarische Psalmenbruchstücke.* Die hexaplarischen Psalmenfragmente der Handschriften Vaticanus graecus 752 und Canonicianus graecus 62. Einleitung, Ausgabe, Erläuterung. XXVIII–446 Seiten. 1975.

Bd. 9   BEAT ZUBER: *Vier Studien zu den Ursprüngen Israels.* Die Sinaifrage und Probleme der Volks- und Traditionsbildung. 152 Seiten. 1976. Vergriffen.

Bd. 10   EDUARDO ARENS: *The HΛΘON-Sayings in the Synoptic Tradition.* A Historico-critical Investigation. 370 Seiten. 1976.

Bd. 11   KARL JAROŠ: *Sichem.* Eine archäologische und religionsgeschichtliche Studie, mit besonderer Berücksichtigung von Jos 24. 280 Seiten, 193 Abbildungen. 1976.

Bd. 11a   KARL JAROŠ/BRIGITTE DECKERT: *Studien zur Sichem-Area.* 81 Seiten, 23 Abbildungen. 1977.

Bd. 12   WALTER BÜHLMANN: *Vom rechten Reden und Schweigen.* Studien zu Proverbien 10–31. 371 Seiten. 1976.

Bd. 13   IVO MEYER: *Jeremia und die falschen Propheten.* 155 Seiten. 1977. Vergriffen.

Bd. 14   OTHMAR KEEL: *Vögel als Boten.* Studien zu Ps 68,12–14, Gen 8,6–12, Koh 10,20 und dem Aussenden von Botenvögeln in Ägypten. – Mit einem Beitrag von Urs Winter zu Ps 56, 1 und zur Ikonographie der Göttin mit der Taube. 164 Seiten, 44 Abbildungen. 1977.

Bd. 15   MARIE-LOUISE GUBLER: *Die frühesten Deutungen des Todes Jesu.* Eine motivgeschichtliche Darstellung aufgrund der neueren exegetischen Forschung. XVI–424 Seiten. 1977. Vergriffen.

Bd. 16   JEAN ZUMSTEIN: *La condition du croyant dans l'Evangile selon Matthieu.* 467 pages. 1977. Epuisé.

Bd. 17   FRANZ SCHNIDER: *Die verlorenen Söhne.* Strukturanalytische und historisch-kritische Untersuchungen zu Lk 15. 105 Seiten. 1977.

Bd. 18   HEINRICH VALENTIN: *Aaron.* Eine Studie zur vor-priesterschriftlichen Aaron-Überlieferung. VIII–441 Seiten. 1978.

Bd. 19   MASSÉO CALOZ: *Etude sur la LXX origénienne du Psautier.* Les relations entre les leçons des Psaumes du Manuscrit Coislin 44, les Fragments des Hexaples et le texte du Psautier Gallican. 480 pages. 1978.

Bd. 20   RAPHAEL GIVEON: *The Impact of Egypt on Canaan.* Iconographical and Related Studies. 156 Seiten, 73 Abbildungen. 1978.

Bd. 21   DOMINIQUE BARTHÉLEMY: *Etudes d'histoire du texte de l'Ancien Testament.* XXV–419 pages. 1978. Vergriffen.

Bd. 22/1 CESLAS SPICQ: *Notes de Lexicographie néo-testamentaire.* Tome I: p. 1–524. 1978. Epuisé.

Bd. 22/2 CESLAS SPICQ: *Notes de Lexicographie néo-testamentaire.* Tome II: p. 525–980. 1978. Epuisé.

Bd. 22/3 CESLAS SPICQ: *Notes de Lexicographie néo-testamentaire.* Supplément. 698 pages. 1982.

Bd. 23   BRIAN M. NOLAN: *The Royal Son of God.* The Christology of Matthew 1–2 in the Setting of the Gospel. 282 Seiten. 1979.

Bd. 24   KLAUS KIESOW: *Exodustexte im Jesajabuch.* Literarkritische und motivgeschichtliche Analysen. 221 Seiten. 1979.

Bd. 25/1 MICHAEL LATTKE: *Die Oden Salomos in ihrer Bedeutung für Neues Testament und Gnosis.* Band I. Ausführliche Handschriftenbeschreibung. Edition mit deutscher Parallel-Übersetzung. Hermeneutischer Anhang zur gnostischen Interpretation der Oden Salomos in der Pistis Sophia. XI–237 Seiten. 1979.

Bd. 25/1a MICHAEL LATTKE: *Die Oden Salomos in ihrer Bedeutung für Neues Testament und Gnosis.* Band Ia. Der syrische Text der Edition in Estrangela Faksimile des griechischen Papyrus Bodmer XI. 68 Seiten. 1980.

Bd. 25/2 MICHAEL LATTKE: *Die Oden Salomos in ihrer Bedeutung für Neues Testament und Gnosis.* Band II. Vollständige Wortkonkordanz zur handschriftlichen, griechischen, koptischen, lateinischen und syrischen Überlieferung der Oden Salomos. Mit einem Faksimile des Kodex N. XVI–201 Seiten. 1979.

Bd. 25/3 MICHAEL LATTKE: *Die Oden Salomos in ihrer Bedeutung für Neues Testament und Gnosis.* Band III. XXXIV–478 Seiten. 1986.

Bd. 26   MAX KÜCHLER: *Frühjüdische Weisheitstraditionen.* Zum Fortgang weisheitlichen Denkens im Bereich des frühjüdischen Jahweglaubens. 703 Seiten. 1979. Vergriffen.

Bd. 27   JOSEF M. OESCH: *Petucha und Setuma.* Untersuchungen zu einer überlieferten Gliederung im hebräischen Text des Alten Testaments. XX–392–37* Seiten. 1979.

Bd. 28   ERIK HORNUNG / OTHMAR KEEL (Herausgeber): *Studien zu altägyptischen Lebenslehren.* 394 Seiten. 1979.

Bd. 29   HERMANN ALEXANDER SCHLÖGL: *Der Gott Tatenen.* Nach Texten und Bildern des Neuen Reiches. 216 Seiten, 14 Abbildungen. 1980.

Bd. 30   JOHANN JAKOB STAMM: *Beiträge zur Hebräischen und Altorientalischen Namenkunde.* XVI–264 Seiten. 1980.

Bd. 31   HELMUT UTZSCHNEIDER: *Hosea – Prophet vor dem Ende.* Zum Verhältnis von Geschichte und Institution in der alttestamentlichen Prophetie. 260 Seiten. 1980.

Bd. 32 PETER WEIMAR: *Die Berufung des Mose*. Literaturwissenschaftliche Analyse von Exodus 2,23–5,5. 402 Seiten. 1980.

Bd. 33 OTHMAR KEEL: *Das Böcklein in der Milch seiner Mutter und Verwandtes*. Im Lichte eines altorientalischen Bildmotivs. 163 Seiten, 141 Abbildungen. 1980.

Bd. 34 PIERRE AUFFRET: *Hymnes d'Egypte et d'Israël*. Etudes de structures littéraires. 316 pages, 1 illustration. 1981.

Bd. 35 ARIE VAN DER KOOIJ: *Die alten Textzeugen des Jesajabuches*. Ein Beitrag zur Textgeschichte des Alten Testaments. 388 Seiten. 1981.

Bd. 36 CARMEL McCARTHY: *The Tiqqune Sopherim and Other Theological Corrections in the Masoretic Text of the Old Testament*. 280 Seiten. 1981.

Bd. 37 BARBARA L. BEGELSBACHER-FISCHER: *Untersuchungen zur Götterwelt des Alten Reiches im Spiegel der Privatgräber der IV. und V. Dynastie*. 336 Seiten. 1981.

Bd. 38 MÉLANGES DOMINIQUE BARTHÉLEMY. *Etudes bibliques offertes à l'occasion de son 60e anniversaire*. Edités par Pierre Casetti, Othmar Keel et Adrian Schenker. 724 pages, 31 illustrations. 1981.

Bd. 39 ANDRÉ LEMAIRE: *Les écoles et la formation de la Bible dans l'ancien Israël*. 142 pages, 14 illustrations. 1981.

Bd. 40 JOSEPH HENNINGER: *Arabica Sacra*. Aufsätze zur Religionsgeschichte Arabiens und seiner Randgebiete. Contributions à l'histoire religieuse de l'Arabie et de ses régions limitrophes. 347 Seiten. 1981.

Bd. 41 DANIEL VON ALLMEN: *La famille de Dieu*. La symbolique familiale dans le paulinisme. LXVII–330 pages, 27 planches. 1981.

Bd. 42 ADRIAN SCHENKER: *Der Mächtige im Schmelzofen des Mitleids*. Eine Interpretation von 2 Sam 24. 92 Seiten. 1982.

Bd. 43 PAUL DESELAERS: *Das Buch Tobit*. Studien zu seiner Entstehung, Komposition und Theologie. 532 Seiten + Übersetzung 16 Seiten. 1982.

Bd. 44 PIERRE CASETTI: *Gibt es ein Leben vor dem Tod?* Eine Auslegung von Psalm 49. 315 Seiten. 1982.

Bd. 45 FRANK-LOTHAR HOSSFELD: *Der Dekalog*. Seine späten Fassungen, die originale Komposition und seine Vorstufen. 308 Seiten. 1982. Vergriffen.

Bd. 46 ERIK HORNUNG: *Der ägyptische Mythos von der Himmelskuh*. Eine Ätiologie des Unvollkommenen. Unter Mitarbeit von Andreas Brodbeck, Hermann Schlögl und Elisabeth Staehelin und mit einem Beitrag von Gerhard Fecht. XII–129 Seiten, 10 Abbildungen. 1982.

Bd. 47 PIERRE CHERIX: *Le Concept de Notre Grande Puissance (CG VI, 4)*. Texte, remarques philologiques, traduction et notes. XIV–95 pages. 1982.

Bd. 48 JAN ASSMANN/WALTER BURKERT/FRITZ STOLZ: *Funktionen und Leistungen des Mythos*. Drei altorientalische Beispiele. 118 Seiten, 17 Abbildungen. 1982.

Bd. 49 PIERRE AUFFRET: *La sagesse a bâti sa maison*. Etudes de structures littéraires dans l'Ancien Testament et spécialement dans les psaumes. 580 pages. 1982.

Bd. 50/1 DOMINIQUE BARTHÉLEMY: *Critique textuelle de l'Ancien Testament*. 1. Josué, Juges, Ruth, Samuel, Rois, Chroniques, Esdras, Néhémie, Esther. Rapport final du Comité pour l'analyse textuelle de l'Ancien Testament hébreu institué par l'Alliance Biblique Universelle, établi en coopération avec Alexander R. Hulst †, Norbert Lohfink, William D. McHardy, H. Peter Rüger, coéditeur, James A. Sanders, coéditeur. 812 pages. 1982.

Bd. 50/2   DOMINIQUE BARTHÉLEMY: *Critique textuelle de l'Ancien Testament.* 2. Isaïe, Jérémie, Lamentations. Rapport final du Comité pour l'analyse textuelle de l'Ancien Testament hébreu institué par l'Alliance Biblique Universelle, établi en coopération avec Alexander R. Hulst †, Norbert Lohfink, William D. McHardy, H. Peter Rüger, coéditeur, James A. Sanders, coéditeur. 1112 pages. 1986.

Bd. 51   JAN ASSMANN: *Re und Amun.* Die Krise des polytheistischen Weltbilds im Ägypten der 18.–20. Dynastie. XII–309 Seiten. 1983.

Bd. 52   MIRIAM LICHTHEIM: *Late Egyptian Wisdom Literature in the International Context.* A Study of Demotic Instructions. X–240 Seiten. 1983.

Bd. 53   URS WINTER: *Frau und Göttin.* Exegetische und ikonographische Studien zum weiblichen Gottesbild im Alten Israel und in dessen Umwelt. XVIII–928 Seiten, 520 Abbildungen. 1983. 2. Auflage mit einem Nachwort, 8 Seiten. 1987.

Bd. 54   PAUL MAIBERGER: *Topographische und historische Untersuchungen zum Sinaiproblem.* Worauf beruht die Identifizierung des Ǧabal Mūsā mit dem Sinai? 189 Seiten, 13 Tafeln. 1984.

Bd. 55   PETER FREI/KLAUS KOCH: *Reichsidee und Reichsorganisation im Perserreich.* 119 Seiten, 17 Abbildungen. 1984

Bd. 56   HANS-PETER MÜLLER: *Vergleich und Metapher im Hohenlied.* 59 Seiten. 1984.

Bd. 57   STEPHEN PISANO: *Additions or Omissions in the Books of Samuel.* The Significant Pluses and Minuses in the Massoretic, LXX and Qumran Texts. XIV–295 Seiten. 1984.

Bd. 58   ODO CAMPONOVO: *Königtum, Königsherrschaft und Reich Gottes in den Frühjüdischen Schriften.* XVI–492 Seiten. 1984.

Bd. 59   JAMES KARL HOFFMEIER: *Sacred in the Vocabulary of Ancient Egypt.* The Term DSR, with Special Reference to Dynasties I–XX. XXIV–281 Seiten, 24 Figures. 1985.

Bd. 60   CHRISTIAN HERRMANN: *Formen für ägyptische Fayencen.* Katalog der Sammlung des Biblischen Instituts der Universität Freiburg Schweiz und einer Privatsammlung. XXVIII–199 Seiten. 1985.

Bd. 61   HELMUT ENGEL: *Die Susanna-Erzählung.* Einleitung, Übersetzung und Kommentar zum Septuaginta-Text und zur Theodition-Bearbeitung. 205 Seiten + Anhang 11 Seiten. 1985.

Bd. 62   ERNST KUTSCH: *Die chronologischen Daten des Ezechielbuches.* 82 Seiten. 1985.

Bd. 63   MANFRED HUTTER: *Altorientalische Vorstellungen von der Unterwelt.* Literar- und religionsgeschichtliche Überlegungen zu «Nergal und Ereškigal». VIII–187 Seiten. 1985.

Bd. 64   HELGA WEIPPERT/KLAUS SEYBOLD/MANFRED WEIPPERT: *Beiträge zur prophetischen Bildsprache in Israel und Assyrien.* IX–93 Seiten. 1985.

Bd. 65   ABDEL-AZIZ FAHMY SADEK: *Contribution à l'étude de l'Amdouat.* Les variantes tardives du Livre de l'Amdouat dans les papyrus du Musée du Caire. XVI–400 pages, 175 illustrations. 1985.

Bd. 66   HANS-PETER STÄHLI: *Solare Elemente im Jahweglauben des Alten Testaments.* X–60 Seiten. 1985.

Bd. 67   OTHMAR KEEL / SILVIA SCHROER: *Studien zu den Stempelsiegeln aus Palästina/Israel.* Band I. 115 Seiten, 103 Abbildungen. 1985.

Bd. 68   WALTER BEYERLIN: *Weisheitliche Vergewisserung mit Bezug auf den Zionskult.* Studien zum 125. Psalm. 96 Seiten. 1985.

Bd. 69   RAPHAEL VENTURA: *Living in a City of the Dead.* A Selection of Topographical and Administrative Terms in the Documents of the Theban Necropolis. XII–232 Seiten. 1986.

Bd. 70   CLEMENS LOCHER: *Die Ehre einer Frau in Israel.* Exegetische und rechtsvergleichende Studien zu Dtn 22,13–21. XVIII–464 Seiten. 1986.

Bd. 71   HANS-PETER MATHYS: *Liebe deinen Nächsten wie dich selbst.* Untersuchungen zum alttestamentlichen Gebot der Nächstenliebe (Lev 19,18). XIV–196 Seiten. 1986.

Bd. 72   FRIEDRICH ABITZ: *Ramses III. in den Gräbern seiner Söhne.* 156 Seiten. 1986.

Bd. 73   DOMINIQUE BARTHÉLEMY/DAVID W. GOODING/JOHAN LUST/EMANUEL TOV: *The Story of David and Goliath.* 160 Seiten. 1986.

Bd. 74   SILVIA SCHROER: *In Israel gab es Bilder.* Nachrichten von darstellender Kunst im Alten Testament. XVI–553 Seiten, 146 Abbildungen. 1987.

Bd. 75   ALAN R. SCHULMAN: *Ceremonial Execution and Public Rewards.* Some Historical Scenes on New Kingdom Private Stelae. 296 Seiten. 41 Abbildungen. 1987.

Bd. 76   JOŽE KRAŠOVEC: *La justice (Ṣdq) de Dieu dans la Bible hébraïque et l'interprétation juive et chrétienne.* 456 pages. 1988.

Bd. 77   HELMUT UTZSCHNEIDER: *Das Heiligtum und das Gesetz.* Studien zur Bedeutung der sinaitischen Heiligtumstexte (Ez 25–40; Lev 8–9). XIV–326 Seiten. 1988.

Bd. 78   BERNARD GOSSE: *Isaie 13,1–14,23.* Dans la tradition littéraire du livre d'Isaïe et dans la tradition des oracles contre les nations. 308 pages. 1988.

Bd. 79   INKE W. SCHUMACHER: *Der Gott Sopdu – Der Herr der Fremdländer.* XVI–364 Seiten. 6 Abbildungen. 1988.

Bd. 80   HELLMUT BRUNNER: *Das hörende Herz.* Kleine Schriften zur Religions- und Geistesgeschichte Ägyptens. Herausgegeben von Wolfgang Röllig. 449 Seiten. 1988.

Bd. 81   WALTER BEYERLIN: *Bleilot, Brecheisen oder was sonst?* Revision einer Amos-Vision. 68 Seiten. 1988.

Bd. 82   MANFRED HUTTER: *Behexung, Entsühnung und Heilung.* Das Ritual der Tunnawiya für ein Königspaar aus mittelhethitischer Zeit (KBo XXI 1 – KUB IX 34 – KBo XXI 6). 186 Seiten. 1988.

Bd. 83   RAPHAEL GIVEON: *Scarabs from recent Excavations in Israel.* 134 Seiten, 12 Seiten Abbildungen. 1988.